THE QUEEN BEE

# BEFORE I WAS BLACK

DOROTHY BEE WILLIAMS

Before I Was Black
Copyright © 2023 by Dorothy Bee Williams

All rights reserved. No part of this publication may be reproduced, distributed, or transmitted in any form or by any means, including photocopying, recording, or other electronic or mechanical methods, without the prior written permission of the author, except in the case of brief quotations embodied in critical reviews and certain other non-commercial uses permitted by copyright law.

ISBN
978-1-960758-31-6 (Paperback)
978-1-960758-32-3 (eBook)

THE QUEEN BEE

# BEFORE I WAS BLACK

## TABLE OF CONTENTS

Foreword ............................................................................................. ix
Introduction ....................................................................................... xi

Chapter 1    Before I Was Black ............................................................. 1
Chapter 2    Becoming Black ................................................................ 21
Chapter 3    Black on Purpose ..............................................................61

Acknowledgements and Gratitude ..................................................... 73

*Dedicated to the Amazing Grace and Tender Mercy of Almighty God, and to My 89-year-old mother "Willie Mae Oatis" of Columbia, Mississippi, for Blessing me with Hope, Courage and the Purpose to be the Best Black I can Possibly Be.*

# FOREWORD

Life is but a journey we partake with the first breath we inhale on this earth. Life is not easy but death is the promise of life. In between life and death, we must strive to make the best of whatever conditions afforded to us. It is not always easy, as complications, adversity and negativity will present itself somewhere along this journey. The power to be great is within us all and it depends on us to survive and make it best as can be. It is my hope that some weary soul will read my story and become uplifted to overcome any and every obstacle. It is my hope that the ones without adversity can share my hope, dreams, and experiences with another, that it be a spark to the flame already inside. There is but one race, and that is the human race and we all are commissioned to love one another despite any differences, and come together as humanity to be the best for each other we can be in unity. Love is what love does and my story is just a story of love.

# INTRODUCTION

Before I Was Black, I was born of the human race, just a biological female with dark complexion skin which now thru evolution and societal influences, I am Woman and I am Black. That makes me a Black Woman. I didn't choose to be a female nor did I choose that my skin be dark; I was born this way. I was also born without a voice and grew up to become an angry Black Woman. Now with over sixty years of black experiences, I am validated with much to say. A journey that has taken me from not wanting to be black, to becoming black, to my today in which I am Black on purpose. Today I have a voice, not a black voice but a multi-faceted voice with much to expose, disclose, share, witness, and to render my truth. Before I Was Black is a chronicle, a story of stories, a personal history of my education in black, a not so common sharing of the many dynamics of this life as I've known it, a black education of sorts, based on true events. It is the diary of a not-so-mad black woman. Before I was Black is not a learned expression into this journey of black, but a living, true witness to the experience of being black in America. It's my calling to share, as it is necessary with all the effort of today to shut out and hide the black journey in America. It is my purpose to share the importance of my black story. This book reflects the ideology, hopes, dreams of the oppressed opportunities I witnessed and is of living proof today just what racist redemption and restoration is, and how it has manifested itself in my life. Freedom, life, liberty and the pursuit of happiness should have been mine at birth as an American Citizen but it was denied and had to be fought for. Though it has been a meandering highway of trial and error, it is my truth of how I came to be who I am today. This is my utterance in this rhythm of humanity. This book is the bible of my black truth. My truth is a truth of old, a truth of separation and poverty, a truth of love and compassion, redemption and restoration. My truth was delivered from bags of lies, books of altered reality and a history of falsehoods dictated and methodically executed throughout our great country in every institution and foundation of America.

Before I Was Black is a disclosure of my truth as a woman born black in America, in Mississippi before desegregation. It is not about racism or pointing fingers but only to document, validate and share my experiences as a black girl not wanting to be black. It reflects my childhood and future desire to become a black woman supporting my existence in the societal definition of what black is. Black defined the rugged paths I had to travel, most unhappy and most, not by choice. All the current attempts to deny our black history being taught in schools and colleges, is that same attempts orchestrated by the same people that kept my people oppressed. Before my time, black people were lynched for learning to read even the Holy Bible. The skin I was born in and any attachments made to it is the reason why I am so black today and why I am today, a beautiful black woman without apology, but "Black on Purpose".

## CHAPTER ONE

# Before I Was Black

*"And ye shall know the truth and
the truth shall set you free"*

Before I was Black, I was just a Negro, born in America with American Parents. Once the schools integrated in Mississippi, I became Black and I did not like it. I didn't like the attachments that came with the word black.

I was once a Negro, but am now a Black American. I have a label and no one asked me about it. No one asked me what I want to be called, but what I know for sure, I didn't want to be Black, as dictated to me. I think I would rather be called Negro more so than Black. Even Nigger is okay with me because it has elevated to Nigga and that's okay. Even today, I oppose being referred to as a Black Woman, a Black American and most certainly an African American Woman...if that's okay. The only color I knew of as a youngster, was the colored folks, them colored people or simply them coloreds, not knowing the reference meant Blacks as a collective, because I wasn't Black, I was Caramel. The only other people I encountered were white folks and there was a vast difference in what that meant as to status in life. I didn't want to be Black but it seemed as if I was trapped because the tan of my skin was God Given at birth, as it was my bloodline, my DNA. I didn't know that my skin tone would create such diverse and troubled roads in which I was destined to travel. If I had a say so in it, I would've been born white and I wouldn't be writing this book as a chronicle of my biological induction into the world of black. It seemed that I was cursed from birth.

Before I was Black, my home state Mississippi was still segregated and it wasn't until the schools integrated in 1970, I realized that I was Black and there were many negative stipulations that came with my black. Having been born on New Year Day, 1959, in a shotgun shack on the banks of the Pearl River, high on a bluff ironically Bluff Street, my black was imperative as was that old black river creeping down the westside of Marion County in Columbia, Mississippi. We were indisputably poor, but my mother was rich in spirit and desired to do better in life, for herself and for her children. She passed that yearning on to her eight children, of which five lived in that shotgun shack with her, and the oldest two living with her parents. Mother placed cement blocks in front of the stove and sink that my sister right above me and I would stand on to help her cook and wash dishes. There was no indoor plumbing, no bathtub, no hot running water but instead a hydrant on the back porch and an enclosed toilet outside on the porch also. We had a number two and five galvanized tin tubs that we bathed in and did the laundry in with a scrub board. It was horrible and I didn't like it yet I didn't know at that time that our living conditions were because we were Negro blacks living in old slave quarters, specifically, Smith Quarters, the place of my birth. Three things I will never forget mainly on my seventh birthday when momma asked me to take the pot with water boiling on it off the ire and when I did the handle turned severely burning my left arm and splashes on my chest. I never said a word but went to the backroom where all the children slept and I was amazed at the mountains of skin that bubbled up on my arm, yet I never said a word. My older sister walked in and saw that I was burnt and she started screaming. Momma couldn't afford to take me to a doctor, so she nursed my arm by salving it and wrapping it up in torn white sheet rags. The memory of that one cement slab between the house and that old river traumatized me every time my mother drove by it because I just knew we were going to go off that embankment and die. Lastly, the memory of me falling out of the car on our way to church one Sunday and almost rolling into the creek and again my sister screamed but I was again, silent. There was no safety place for me in Smith Quarters, as I had already learned how to internalize my pain and I carried much of this pain into my adult life.

This pain was smothered in blackness and it had no voice. My voice was hushed and stifled in the blackness of my journey and destination.

Before I Was Black, my mother, a single mother, worked long hard hours even weekends and yet we were poor, distressed, depressed and oppressed. We lived in a small world on an embankment above the Pearl River, with gravel roads, dust, and the city dump down the street as our playground. A pickle plant wobbled on the hill across from our shack, and a slaughter pen also up the road, and it was our only interaction with whites unless we went to town. Everything was labeled, colored laundry mats, colored public drinking fountains at the courthouse and we had only one colored school inside the city limits, with grades one thru twelve enrolled at that small school, John J. Jefferson High School, the Mighty Green Waves, as it was at that time. This school had great educators as I recall, and I was an A student, having started school at the age of five, but I was from the river banks on the other side of the tracks, therefore I was less important, and not called upon too often. A few of the teachers recognized my intelligence and groomed it so to speak at Jefferson. I acquired numerous great memories especially times when I would skip in the lunch line so I could stand behind the senior class, specifically Walter Payton and the other tall good looking young black men who are mostly deceased now. Jefferson fashioned talent shows on Fridays with everyone in attendance and this memory is priceless.

In my memory bank is a file that pictures dear old friends and classmates including Walter Payton, up on stage in the school gym singing and dancing to the songs of yesterday, but most of them are now gone. Some of the teachers there were very mean and when students acted up in class, including myself, one teacher would stand us up in a row, in front of the class to go across our knees with a wooden paddle or wooden guns used for plays. The paddle had three holes in it and had engraved on it "The Board of Education". It seemed to be my closest friend as I stayed in trouble and had many fights there. My classmates fought often at school with many bullies to contend, but I was a fighter too and would find myself on the toilet getting jumped on, even though it is funny today, it was not funny at the time. I will never forget how one classmate, who became a good friend still, ripped my bandages off my burned arm, and momma had to doctor it all over again as the scabbing had been ripped off as well.

Back in those days, we planned our fights, put chips on our shoulders and drew lines in the dirt to start the fight. Yet the next day or so, we were all still friends and have remained friends now, for over fifty-five years. My older sister had to come to my rescue a few times, when others would try and catch me alone and double team me, but she would show up and kick their butts. Today, there are teeth imprints from a fight with a girl who was much taller than me, who clenched my shoulder in her teeth and tattooed me for life. This had to be a black thing, yet I did not understand it, nor did I know where black people got the propensity for violence, but now I do. I've read the history books and learned it instigated from the same violence put upon us in years past and even unto today, It truly is a black thang.

Before I was Black, I was ashamed, broken, confused, angry, sad and already damaged, not yet ten years old and a black nobody. The first black woman I saw on our little black and white television that seemed to have what I desired was Diana Ross, and I wanted to be like her, for she was surrounded by white and dressed in white. White inferred purity and light and it was a good thing and seemed to be a good thing to be or become. White people had other names too, just as I, but they are irrelevant and warrant no credit to my black story. All things I knew associated with white beheld a real good label and I wanted to have it. White was right, the light, purity, white milk, white Sunday shoes, white schools, white doctors, the good doctors, so on and so forth. Even the light bulb in the ceiling was white and ironically gave light to black surroundings. My story is not seeking sympathy or even empathy, for those days are long gone in some respects, but the memories created are for a lifetime and every day I thank God for every memory. It was unbeknownst to me that one day in my future, I would lose countless memories in a brain tumor when it was removed, but that also, one day my memories would help keep me vital, alive, and happy, as at times, they are all I have. Life has brought about many changes as family and friends aren't what they used to be and black neighborhoods are not collective like they used to be. One day, I knew this black that I was, would have to change and be accepted by myself and others, in order for me to grow to become a somebody, and not just black. I was born great having started school at the age of five, I was already an artist, very bright and eager. There were no headstart or kindergarten programs for us, yet I went to school with hunger as it also provided a great escape from my life on the river banks. Being smart worked to my advantage as I believed it set me apart and made me feel better about myself and it brought a smile to my face. We had great teachers at our little black school and I pursued my education with pure passion. The dictionary was my best friend and playmate while comic books challenged my gift in drawing as I mirrored with pencil on paper anything I could find, various characters from my favorite comic books to include Superwoman and Veronica from the Archie comic books. Cutting the characters in half and drawing the other half until I got it identical as in the book, was like sunshine on dark cloudy black days. With no talent to showcase at the talent shows at school, I probed deeper into my books and my love for drawing, but in years to come, my artworks would showcase themselves and give me great pleasure and accolades. It still felt like I could only do what I was told to do and I had no voice or feelings yet, just little black girl conceptions and responses.

Before I Was Black my mother eventually found another shotgun shack further south on South Main Street across the tracks again, with downtown Columbia, the City of Charm north of us. Nothing about my community and my city was charming to me, but rather, quite alarming and full of despair. We were not on the riverbank anymore but across the street from it and the houses on the west side of the street had that black river peeping in their backdoors and it was more than spooky to look out my neighbors back doors with a river crawling so nearby. We were nothing more than Negroes, colored, and of course niggers, living in the slums in a black ghetto way of life. The thing about shotguns shacks that caused me boundless fear, was the ability to look through the front door and see out the back door. This new house was another shack sitting on cements blocks and was soon lifted off those blocks when Hurricane Camille made her debut in 1968. All the windows were blown out of that shack and half the roof came off, as we huddled in a corner under a blanket, as my mother had chosen to ride out the storm sheltered in place. I learned a lot in that neighborhood, they called it the Hole and yet it was filled with a variety of black people. Some were business owners with a restaurant like the Blue Flame, Ms. Cheese convenience store, Lonnie Butler barber shop, Ms. Christel Bell beauty shop and Lula Mae's juke joint. Mother was strict, reserved, very spiritual and she didn't permit us to stray far from home. On Sundays, us kids from our hood would walk up the street to the movie theater of which blacks were not allowed on the ground floor, but could watch movies from the balcony. But by the Grace of God, that eventually had to change as I imagined the whites below grew tired of blacks pouring drinks on top of their heads and even being urinated on, as a measure of our compromise and it was funny to me. We were raised in church and our new shack sat right next to a True Vine Baptist Church where I was baptized. I'm most thankful today, that I was raised in church and introduced to the Word of God at a young age or I probably wouldn't have made it thus far today. Mother did not drink, smoke or party and she was a Madea, as she had no problem whipping the tar off our behinds. I laugh now, but pain had already injected its sting in my heart and body. I hated whippings and got plenty of them because I was what they called "bad". We were sheltered and not allowed to go roaming in the Hole, but every chance I got, I was where I shouldn't be. I learned to party there, but it was a poor party, on the porch of those shacks' kind of party. drink liquor and beer in the back yard kind of party. In the Hole, I learned that it was okay to call a woman a bitch and not get beat up. It was a black thing but today everyone does it. Not me. Even though I don't frequent those areas anymore, I'm not sure how I would react to being called a bitch or a nigger. Once I started to become black later on, I would react with violence and somehow prove that I was a nigger and even more so, a bitch. A black bitch.

Before I Was Black, it was years later mother bought a house in an area called Webb Quarters and this house had a bathtub, hot and cold running water and a yard to play in. Ironically, it was at this same time frame that the schools fully integrated and I started ninth grade high school in a white school, Columbia High School in the year 1972 and it also seemed to be the end of the colored labels on public facilities. Soon I had to become Black no matter how I detested being black, as it was inevitably a part of me that I could not change. My feelings were mostly black because I was not allowed to feel, just to react. Just like those piercing eyes in the trees in the back of our shotgun shack staring at me waiting to lure me toward that old black river Pearl, I had been taught to stay away from that river because blacks had been killed and found on the riverbanks and I had been taught not to trust white, the same white I would fatefully pursue. Our new home was far from that old black river Pearl, but in April 1983, that river came close to our new home when it flooded Marion County, as though it was still looking for me. It seemed I couldn't get away far enough from that river as it consumed the entire southern portion of our neighborhood including Highway 98 where it engulfed whole bridges. It was like a giant lake had reformed our community and my siblings and I swam and played in those waters that swallowed up Duckworth Park. I was full of fear about everything around me, my environment was full of black holes that could easily gulp me up and cast me on the riverbanks. Nobody ever asked me what I wanted to be called, I often felt like those black cows I could hear squealing as they were slaughtered for their beef and sold at the slaughter pen in Smith Quarters where I was born. It wasn't my skin color I did not want; it was the oppression put upon me having been labeled black, because I had beautiful skin, all creamy and light brown, even golden at times. I was not going to grow up black, for black was a stain on my heart, a smothering of my spirit.

Before I was Black, the word itself implicated something not respectable, of no value, something ugly, scary and to be avoided. That black cat, the infamous black cloud, black balls, black heart, black fingers, the Black Plague, and the infamous little black sheep. That black ass lie was notorious and cruel, as it incited dire consequences. There was also blackmail, the blacklist, black tar, the black eye and of course black snakes. Blackberries was the only black I could relate to that was appealing. Even black coffee was bitter but more flavorful with white milk. I didn't want to be a part of the black theater, the black orchestra, the black anything, I had no foresight that in the future, that same Black would still be a negative as reflected in a societal specific and inevitably it was still racist. Racism was different in my youth as opposed to what it is today as it was openly expressed, rude, fearful, and dangerous. We knew what lines not to cross, as racism was a violent expression upon my people, without limitations when we were yet Negroes. The civil rights movement was a lifesaver and the desegregation of public schools was an act of God. Now, some sixty years later Black is yet seeking more civil rights and liberties that had previously been afforded to only a certain group of people, and it denied my people access to a higher quality of living. Today we're having Black Lives Matter protests, and our prisons are filled with our black men all over the country. The police kill our black men and some women and just get a slap on the wrist. If George Floyd was white and the police who killed him were black, they all would be dead. I never would've believed that the core of our government would be attacked by the same kind of people that constructed its laws. Many laws and amendments of our Constitution that oppressed blacks and were designed to elevate and keep private the access to a better life are still in place today. Yet, I look at how many blacks, especially the ones with a voice assert themselves and I can see the mindset of old slavery days is still at work. Blacks are deemed a violent people but no one researches the violence put upon us in our efforts for freedom and equal rights. Our greatness was stifled in the mind long ago being some of our ancestors had to bow down to a certain white even when that white was wrong. It's not a genetic mutation but a learned behavior to beat or kill someone just to get what 's demanded of them. To assume one person is better than the next man because of circumstances or status in life including skin color, is a mistake and involuntary genocide. When slavery existed, it was common for slave owners and masters of the plantations to beat and or subject their slaves to severe punishments for whatever reason they desired. It was engraved in the minds of many blacks that greatness only came, with the permission of a white society and that violence was acceptable. Yet today, everything I own and have access to, has to be signed off somewhere along the way by a white man. All the dotted lines, fine print, red tapes and protocol were not designed for my benefit. The system seemed to be against me and the hurdles I had to jump were much higher than that of white society. These words did not come from thought but from actual experiences, therefore with actual and true conclusions. Some sixty years later, I am still defending my black, still trying to be that assertive, productive and prosperous citizen that the Constitution supposedly affords. The label of being the first back to do anything great is racist and Black History Month is appalling because we as a people have been great and have made historical accolades long before we were afforded freedom from slavery and awarded the right to vote. In my heart and spirit, I know that if the people who assaulted the White House were primarily black, the outcome would've been a massacre. The white that dictated a bias government, rules and regulations of all our institutions, is the same white that attacked the seat of America. I didn't know that one day America would start to look like true America with people who look like me in the front seats of our government and commerce society. This might be a black observation, as we still have many more black rows to hoe to become totally equal in all our institutions, markets and functions as a nation. Our nation however, will never be black enough, though at most times it has been very gloomy, black and threatening.

Before I Was Black, America was that white man with silver gray hair, that probably owned a few slaves or had that black nanny in the kitchen and yet still, the same man that stole my virginity and my ability to birth children. It is the same man who denies equal access so that we, black people can become and live as prosperous as they. Just as when blacks move into white neighborhoods, the whites move out and you know the rest of the story. The same white man that signs all the dotted lines that give access to any institution in our county is also the one who calls me an angry black woman when I address these truths. I was and, in some ways, will always be that angry black woman, if that's what it takes to share the truth of my black. I am she, and was she before I was black. The difference is we can openly talk about it today without fear of lynching. Lynching has a new presentation today as the introduction of crack to my people killed and destroyed many families in various ways. Black communities and neighborhoods were much more unified and on one accord than they are today. We were all we had and we had to stick together. Now that we have greater liberties of life, like cell phones, iPads, internet and nice cars, we have divided greatly. We don't have a leader like Dr. Martin Luther King, and the leaders today aren't what they should be. There has been great assault on morals, integrity and standards in our governing majority and even in the church and especially amongst our people of black. My story is about my truth, my black and my being in my varied environments and everyday life. I didn't want this black struggle or the need for another man's permission to become something other than just black. Negroes were just trying to make it and make it better in life. Looks like we did to a certain extent, as I can safely tell my little black story without any little black repercussions. Back in the day, the late 60s, to be black was to be trouble, under constant scrutiny especially in stores and businesses. It stimulated my rebellious spirit and soon the description of nigger in the early Webster dictionary fit me perfectly. Poverty forced me to a new and different way of getting me, me. Ironically, though, I was born a thief and stealing was second nature, as my mother told me when I was an adult in jail for shoplifting, that I'd been stealing since I was a little girl. I jokingly replied to her that she should've gotten me some help sooner, some counseling maybe, but she didn't find that funny. Sticky black fingers committing crimes, stealing and lying about it before the age of ten. Yep! I was a nigger. My engagements on the negative side of the law started young but that's still to come. Momma whippings kept me in line pretty much until I stop feeling pain. Pain was black, and it was a darkness hard to escape with there being so many sources of pain. It was too, like that old black Pearl River creeping by the neighborhood, you couldn't see it especially at night but you could sense it's presence. Pearl was the biggest black snake I've ever seen as a youngster and that wasn't just a black thing.

Before I was Black, I didn't know love or what love looked like in my small feeble black mind. I heard Jesus loved me and I had absolutely no comprehension of that either. I never heard the word used in daily life, or on the dusty dirt gravel roads we traveled daily. The roads weren't black with tar, but pebbled with little stones of defeat and they all led to that old black river or ran parallel to it. Even that black dirty dumpsite right down below on the banks was black and when we played in it, the bottom of our feet were black. This black thing was getting the best of me long before I was black. I was learning much too early that love was not genetically obtained and not a product of my socially inducted blackness. In many ways I wanted to learn what black was until I grew up black and changed my mind. Just a young girl I under the age of twelve, I already understood completely that the reason we were in poverty in that shack above that old black snaky river was because of our skin color. As destiny would have it, I had to become, want and desire my black. A mighty task was before me before I became black. It was most unclear to me that I had already been defined and given a status in life, dictated by a people who thought they were superior to me. Not knowing the true atrocities of my ancestors seeking freedom, and how their sacrifices paved a way for me, I also in return, did know that my black would one day become beautiful. My black was destined as an ugliness in a society of "We the People". I was not one of "The People". In countless years to come even unto this day, my black is not by choice and apparently not the choice of the established white society.

With so much to learn before I even wanted to become black, I knew the black struggle was unavoidable and I had a hard-times black ahead of me.

Before I Was Black, my black didn't write books or produce movies about tree lynchings, but instead, blacks suffered that reality of which movies become blockbusters. Our history of dying trying to read the bible or other books are made great in film but the sting of the truth they are based on, still lingers. What has happened in black communities with battles of racism, injustice, and inequality is not made up, these ain't no jokes, this is not entertainment, just black reality. Black material is hot material today especially the material based on truth and true events. Not many of us are left that survived our black history of not so long ago, that can still tell the story having lived through its' truth. I am commanded to share my truth by a supreme spiritual being, not just for the sake of writing a book. The Word of God says that we will know the truth and the truth will set us free. Let us all be free and acknowledge truth, at least. With efforts being made to erase the journey of our black history, including the realism of racism, we must continue to document our truth and our fights for equal rights. All I had to do growing up was to make it to another day, and to do as I was told. We were created to love one another, to be loved and to share love with all of God's creations, including Mother Nature, and ultimately with God. Love was not a common word in my youth and I had to learn its meaning and how to love myself. The knowledge that I had been created in the image of God and that life was promised to be more abundant for me was foreign language. Black life was a negative before I was born, implanting in my spirit anger, sadness, oppression and hunger. I was born broken and longed for something better than Black. I wanted to be a part of the greater, the abundant and the free. I wanted to get away from black, especially that old black river, the mighty Pearl ominously gazing at me from way down below. I just knew that river with the black waters was going to kidnap me one day but it showed its face in a dream many future nights to come. Black was the nigger I was destined to become and had shadowed my frail undeveloped mindset at a very young age. Once I learned to read, the Webster dictionary was key to my education as its definition of nigger was a forewarning of what I was to become. Before the age of ten, I was already a thief, full of lies, sneaky and deceitful. Yet, I had seen with my own eyes what effect the word had on colored folks as we were called accordingly, but with unpleasant reactions to it. Self-preservation is the key to life but already I wanted to die in the cruel environment I was becoming accustomed to. That shotgun shack with holes in the floors and walls were given to me as a little black gift to speak, but it was not what I wanted, it was a curse. With my momma working day and night, I didn't understand the poverty and anguish we were exposed to in youth, much too young to be crippled as such. I didn't know much as a young child but I quickly learned the problem in my world was my black skin and somehow it had to change. Not the skin but black conditions.

Before I was Black, I was very ugly, felt ugly and everything surrounding me was ugly until I saw Diana Ross on the little black and white television we had acquired and that offered me hope that I could be like her. She was who I wanted to be with the big hair, big eyes, nice clothing, and people surrounding her with love and adoration. It was love that I sought and simple acceptance and yes, a black Cadillac accordingly. The perks afforded to whites, just like the indulgences I saw on that black and white television, was my desire and wishful thinking. Television opened my eyes to a hope and desire for something other than black and all the provocations black represented. That slaughterhouse on the hill proved witness to my propensity to steal, as my sticky little fingers would steal those fudgesicles in that freezer and bubblegum off that counter every time I went there. I had to have one and it was good too, before I was black and before I got caught stealing them. That slaughterhouse, where they killed cows and sold that good meat, with racks of potato chips, candies and a freezer full of ice cream bars introduced me the one of the worst whippings ever when the owner told my mother he caught me stealing. I knew pain and misery long before I knew I was black. It seemed that my fear was innate and demonic with great trials, errors and unescapable aftermaths. The back entrance to a narrow black hallway up raggedy black stairs we had to climb just to see a doctor, was frightening, as very few doctors took the colors in. Before I was black my black life was yet isolated and black, meaning without. The colored hot dog stands where we had to sit way in a back room was offensive and the wooden plank floors were even blacker, and offered no measure of escape. These occasions had no sense of hope but were very intriguing to me as it left me feeling outcast, alien and not of this world. They left me feeling black.

Before I was Black, I wanted to be white. I wanted that white respect that came with it and I wanted my black life to be better. The oppression and poverty of the black life was not destined for me. The white I saw worked important jobs, behind the counters and required money for services denied to us. The only white I knew worked at the banks and front offices while black women like my mother, cleaned their floors, cooked their meals, scrubbed their toilets, and nursed their babies. Service work was not for me and already I knew I had to find another way to prosperity. It was greatly my desire to be the first black to survive the ghetto and move up in the world. Black girl magic was what I needed. It would take some kind of magic to get me from the other side of the railroad tracks into a new light of success. It was obvious that the blacks who lived south of the tracks were treated differently than the blacks near Jefferson School and they seemed to prosper more and were more accepted than we. I felt trapped in my dictated realm of life on the back black side of the tracks and I knew before I would become black I had to move to the other black side of this same track. I wasn't black. Who said I was black because I was a slightly toasted yellow kind of brown. My mom said when I was born, she stood accused of having a white baby because I was born high yellow, as older folks would say back then. I would rather have been labeled brown instead of black. Within the black community, your shade of black roughly affected your status quo as well and it made me feel adopted. Nothing about being black appealed to me at all. The raggedy shotgun shacks were painful and offered no hope for a better future. I wanted to be like the whites with indoor plumbing, bathrooms with bathtubs, hot and cold running water, plenty of food to eat, and with a new language or vocabulary. They had Christmas parties, a momma and daddy with loving sisters and brothers, family vacations, money, nice cars filled with gas, fine shoes, stylish clothing, school buses and a public library like the Shelby Memorial Library in the white neighborhood.

Before I was Black, my environment was belligerent and the black men about town were even more aggressive as most of them were poor, alcoholic, stinky and threatening, with children out of wedlock all over town, and I didn't want no part of them. Memory fails to share with me any sinister events with the black men of my youth, yet I felt a negative history someplace with them. Something ugly had happened at some time or another, tainting my image of black men. Nothing I was exposed to felt right nor was it inviting, especially that old Pearl River staring at me from down below. That river was too black and the stories I heard about that river were black and the banks of the Pearl were even blacker. The city dump rested on its border and was bursting with black, discarded, burnt and blemished trash full of curiosity and wonder worth plundering. Chances of changing my black label were void and one day I would have to become black not knowing that the white I was pursing, would also become black one day. When white people attacked the White House in recent years I knew we were in trouble and my black as dictated by society didn't stand a chance in hell. It seemed that the white that was right, the ones that constructed our government, was now acting like the black I didn't want to be. When the white public schools first integrated and whites attended our little black school, I sat behind a white boy with long dark hair and clear blue green eyes and I thought I loved him. I wrote him a letter of my love and he gave it to the teacher who contacted my mother and again, I got the worse beatings of my life. When I learned she knew about it, I took a whole bottle of Bayer's aspirin to offset the pain but it didn't work, yet now in hindsight, I was already fated to experiment with drugs. At school I sat next to whites in class, observing them with great scrutiny and I became friends with many at Jefferson School where I received my first eight years of education. The different variations of blondes with blue eyes, brunettes with brown eyes, and the great level of intelligence my new white classmates possessed boggled my little black mind. Being the youngest of my classmates having started school at the age of five, I was ignorant and so naive but I wanted to be smart like them and I wanted my own checkbook too. Yet, I was already smart, a straight A student with a good hand in drawing, but my smart was different, creative and gifted but without an educated vocabulary and this stimulated my affinity for the dictionary and a more superior level of knowledge. My vocabulary was ghetto and black, full of culture and mispronunciations. Momma said because of this, I played inside most times. She said one day while I was inside drawing characters from the comic books, with my siblings outside playing with neighboring children on a wagon with some pulling and others riding the wagon, a car came crushing down the hill. The car rolled downhill from the pickle plant and barreled into the children playing with the wagon, pinning my younger sister under a back tire. She said my auntie in sheer strength and the grace of God lifted that tire off my sister's head, probably saving her life. I was grateful to be inside that day and I will never forget that day. While playing inside, my favorite toy was an Etch-a-Sketch and I spent hours on it trying to draw everything I saw both physically and imaginatively and it provided me a great escape. Seeds of creative expression were planted in my youthful spirit during this time, as I am today a master artist with a degree in fine arts. A new world was on the horizon as I was becoming of age and started having feelings I couldn't identify, but I soon learned that I just wanted some love and eventually, a white love. Romantic notions, puppy love and such evaded my thoughts as I only felt an attraction to men, after the schools integrated. What I was seeking turned out to be the core element of what this old world seeks and that's the feeling of being loved. One day I would learn, experience and embrace love from my own black man but it would be in distant years to come. Black love as I had received thus far, was extraneous and full of injured curiosity as it was also burdened, famished, empty, and so very unattractive. Black love was poor and Black love was unreliable. Black love was petrifying.

Before I was Black most of my memories would delete themselves, leaving me with the recollection of only a few episodes and they were mostly smothered in agony and gloom. Events with my family are scattered and not organized, but family was all I had and my family was everything, as we were unified and stood strong together, which made my mother very happy. Memories of picking blackberries on the train trussell in Smith Quarters and visiting our elders with momma on Sundays after church are pleasant memories from the late sixties and early seventies. Momma was committed to our family accord, unlike today when at times family can be the enemy or act like an enemy. She made sure we were provided for and she wanted us to have healthier experiences than the ones she survived living in poverty and her bad choices of men. She didn't have much affection trying to raise a house full of children but I never believed she had experienced real and true love with any of her husbands. Years later my mom and I discussed my upbringing and we both shared how we felt and I acquired a better understanding of why she beat us so. Momma was a Madea to speak, a very strong authoritarian and her whippings were not normal and but very abusive, but that's what she knew and had received herself as a youngster. A person can't give or share with you something that they don't have is what my pastor at my hometown church, Friendship M.B. Church, often said. Yet, I knew I had to get away somehow. Those whippings imparted to me a flee or fight attitude and façade which caused me to run away eventually and certainly to self-medicate. These experiences and episodes of black culture were extreme and much too black for me. The neighborhoods of my youth, helped raised each other's children and kept a watchful eye on them, as neighborhoods were one big family in the days gone by. They helped the children, kept them straight and would whip you when caught doing wrong and then tell your mother who would whip you again. There weren't many role model men or father figures in our families, most men I was familiar with, had a bottle of liquor in their hands or in their back pocket. My mother was and still is a good woman who raised us up in church. I was baptized at ten years old at True Vine Church on South Main Street, across from that old black river Pearl. Most functions and activities at the church included us, and this quality, I am most grateful for. We all sang in the choir, learned to usher, attended bible study and vacation bible school in the summer when we didn't have to work in the fields picking peas, cucumbers and other vegetables. If my mother was a loose woman drinking, partying and such; I wouldn't have made it today. Black women have been mostly raising their own children since I can remember unlike nowadays, as it seems men are being more active in their children's lives than before, which is awesome. I really don't know why I was a miserable child and unhappy but I found great joy trying to draw and read the dictionary. Finding happiness and peace was my ultimate goal and to not be drowned in the sea of blackness.

Before I was Black, I had a bigma who was my great great auntie and she raised my father J.L. Ishman, as I was his only child as far as I knew. The story was that my father went to prison for stealing watermelons and changed his name to Larry Jones when he was released, then I was born later on as Dorothy Bee Jones but I am an Ishman. Bigma lived in a community called Hardwood Quarters with rows of shotgun shacks on Highway 13 South. Later in life, I learned that all the quarters we live in, were old slave quarters and thus consumed with poverty. My father was killed when he was a young man only 33 years old having been stabbed right below his heart by a white man as my bigma told me. He died two days later and mother took me to see him in the hospital before he died as I vaguely remember the funeral but I was already familiar with great loss and pain. Black pain. My father and mother were not married as she met him while picking nuts from the tung trees that was used to make tung oil and they lived together but she said he was very abusive when he drank liquor. She said when he ran out of liquor, he would drink rubbing alcohol or Dr. Tichenor's and then the whole neighbor had to run and get out of his way. Smith Quarters where I was born on Bluff Street right above the city dump no longer exists. The community and neighborhood of shotgun shacks are long gone along with the city dump. pickle plant and slaughterhouse and is now Bluff Street Park. History as I knew it was a hard pill to swallow but history is knowledge and affords gratitude to my position today. As I have since learned what my ancestors, grandparents and parents endured to help us get to a better place as a people, I am eternally thankful. I used to visit these areas with my pained memories and am today as afraid of that old black river as I was when I was a child living above it. There was a friend of my mother who is now gone that every time she saw me, she would tell me the story of how one day my drunken father was chasing my mother with me in my mother's arms. She said my mother slipped and fell but she said that I never touched the ground, because she caught me and my father could not catch her. She laughed hard when she told me this amazing story and I felt a kinship to her, as she probably saved my life. It's astounding what people do when they are drunk and alcohol seemed to be favored by black men in my neighborhood. Apparently, my father had another woman that he visited and her side piece, a white man was there the day he went over there drunk and that man, bigma said, stabbed my father when they got into a fight. I vaguely knew this man but he was well known and owned property in the hood and rented out many shacks in the quarters. Soon I would realize that many black women had a white man who helped them financially and under cover. There are not many memories I have of my father and I have but one picture of him my bigma gave me and he was tall, handsome, with hazel eyes, curly hair and she said he was part creole and he was alcoholic. Mother said he loved to fight her when he was drunk which caused her great duress, especially when she became pregnant with me. She often reminded me that she died twice trying to bring me into this world as I was eleven pounds, five ounces and it was New Year Day, 1959 in hard time Mississippi. Just the thought of momma giving birth to seven children in that raggedy, but clean, little shack still gives me the jitters. An incredibly strong and determined woman my mother was indeed and I embrace everything I learned from her especially through all the hardships. She told me many times how my father would pick me up as an infant while drunk and fall with me and even how he swung at her one time while she was holding me. He missed her head but knocked the fire out of me and I was just a baby. My momma said he was a very clean man and could sing like an angel as he did sing with a gospel group, The Columbia Jubilees. The leader of that group was a blind man who had a little store off the highway in Hardwood Quarters. He could count money just by rubbing his fingers across it which was amazing to me. Momma kept her shacks spotless and I'm thankful she passed on that trait to me and it may be the reason why she was attracted to my father. He was also a Korean War Veteran so it was in my makeup to eventually join the military. Some fifty years later, after brain surgery with a shaved my head, and scars on my scalp, I understood where the scars may have come from as an infant and including injuries to my head as an adult. I probably will never know why I am prone to and plagued with brain tumors with three growing on my brain this very day, but I often think it is because of all the head trauma and injuries. Sounds pretty bleak and oh so black to me but this is my black story and not a cry of black imaginations.

Before I Was Black, most children had a bigma, auntie or grandma somewhere that helped in their upbringing and I loved my bigma. With her in her brick textured tar sided house off Highway 13 South, I had my own room there, and she spoiled me as much as she could, even growing rows of strawberries in her field, just for me. She had an outhouse too and I hated and was afraid of that outhouse. With those big spiders up in the corners above and that big stinky hole you had to sit on, I rarely made it to the outhouse but there was a peach tree near the outhouse that I did most of my business. You can say I kept it fertilized and that might be why those little tight peaches were so hard. She had one stillbirth which she buried in a shoebox underneath her house, and she warned me of ghosts and hanks that stayed around the bridge past her home. She had many fearful stories that kept me close to her home and out of the woods behind the house.

Spending most weekends and the summer with her when school was out made me feel special in that I had something that was entirely my own. Visiting with bigma was my escape as she was old, she chewed Beechnut tobacco and drank Budweiser beer almost daily. We would sit around her woodstove and watch television and she sometimes cooked our meals on that same stove. Across the highway a skating rink was built, and it was there I first remember being curious and engaging with the black boys as I would sneak over there while she was asleep and this is where I lost my reserves. Before long, I had boyfriends and experimented with sex right there on her front porch in the darkness of night. With no memory of ever being a virgin, I was born guilty and without restraints. One of my great uncles that visited grandma frequently would bring me ice cream and boiled peanuts which I loved both, and while I was standing there eating them, he would run his fingers under my dress and play the piano on my private parts and I let him. I didn't know it was wrong and it caused me great guilt and shame later on in life, but also confirmed that I was never a virgin. Bigma whom I treasured, lived next door to a construction company where this white man worked and he would wave at me when I played outside or sat on the back porch. I would wave back until one day he called me over and tried to have sex with me but I got away and I will always remember the look on his face as he was very disappointed and frustrated as I ran away. I didn't know what I was doing and, there was no love in it and I wanted love, yet I didn't know what love was nor what it looked like. My Bigma became senile and would chase me all over that house screaming the floor was sinking and she would whip me for eating oranges off the tree when there was no orange tree. The final straw broke one morning when she went to whip me because there were ants in the grits I had cooked on her woodstove, but they weren't ants, it was the speckles in the grits. I had to run away from there and got in trouble for running away, as my mother thought I was being fast in the ass. Bigma had to go live with my father's mother who lived in St. Louis but moved back to Mississippi to take care of my bigma. She died when she was ninety-eight years old and I was eighteen, in Europe at that time, serving my country, trying to be black. It was not my knowledge that while I lived in Germany, I would meet a new kind of black, a black that I liked, a black that I had to introduce myself to in order to survive. From infancy to my adolescent years, life was hard, depressed and seemed hopeless. Life had to become more uplifting and I needed a light to shine upon me to show me a better easier way and to guide me to a better outlook. The road thus far was overwhelming and sticky like the black tar on the bottom of my black feet. Why did black have to be so ugly and why could I not be just brown and beautiful. On every side of town where I'd been born and raised, black life was offensive and constraining. My black didn't matter to anyone and it was distressing to my spirit. Black was tacky.

## BLACK GIRL SURVIVE

I been lied on, spied on, died on and cried on, been flipped, dipped, milked and stripped, but I am Black Girl and I will survive.

I been poked, choked, stroked and hoaxed, been used, abused, misconstrued and a fool yet I am Black Girl and I will survive.

I been fly, spry, high and nigh, been shy, that cutie with the black eye, been denied and fried but I am Black Girl, I will survive.

I been up, I been down, I been to hell and underneath the ground, been lazy, crazy, glazed and hazy, a Black Girl born to survive.

I been poor, been rich, sleeping in shacks and sleeping in the ditch, been a witch with a clit, all split with sassy hips, I will Survive.

I been midnight mud and morning dew, I've had plenty and I've had few, been bled, almost dead, stitches in my head but I am all Black Girl and I will survive.

I been nothing, I been all, I been a rebel without cause, I been supplied with creative lies, been despised with no compromise, I been disappointed yet anointed and yet, I am Black Girl and I Survive.

CHAPTER TWO

# Becoming Black

*"Trust in the Lord and Lean Not
to Thine Own Understanding"*

Becoming Black was extremely difficult but absolutely necessary. The schools were now completely integrated and I was surrounded by a white that was new and very exciting to me. I wanted white. The new white had a primary, elementary and high school all separate schools, libraries, friends with benefits and the access to all things more beautiful. Pursuing that white brought about much trouble for me yet ironically it invoked me to discover my own greatness too. Determined to prove the greatness within, I had yet to learn the differences of how to present myself in private and in public environments. I got along well with my fellow honor students at school, but yet I partied with the wild bunch having to find out the hard way that they don't coincide together, and that I couldn't be both. My rebel spirit leaned toward the wild bunch and I already knew I could never be any kind of good girl. The privilege of being a good girl was stolen from me way too young and I no longer could apply for the elite status, damaged already being both black and poor. No matter how bright and smart I was, I lived across the tracks, and in the ghetto. Shame and guilt were not upon my spirit yet, in my quest for greatness and whiteness but in years to come, it caused great internal conflict as I was misunderstood and definitely, a black sheep. Shame and guilt are both monsters, that rape you of your own personal greatness and will serve as a black cloud overhead everywhere you go, if you don't address it and let it consume you. So many curiosities I had in the new black and white Mississippi were never satisfied and I longed for clarity and innocence. Several of my experiences with both white and black men, were devious, and kept secret because they were tailed with danger had I exposed them. Many situations I got myself into as a young black girl kept me in trouble especially with the law. At times hanging out with my white friends, the police would show up and run my white friends off and take me to jail. Most times I went to jail without any charges other than hanging out amongst the whites at night. I was barely fourteen years old, in jail with hardcore criminals but some of them knew me and my family and they watched over me. Most of those men are gone now but a few remain that can attest to this barbarism, as the police would even remove the lightbulb in my cell, leaving me in total darkness. The police would keep me in jail long as they wanted and I never understood how they could get away with that, but I also knew no one would come to get me. Black people were afraid of the law during those days and maybe this is why my mom asked no questions but was glad to see me make it back home. In due course I was sent to the Columbia Training School for juvenile delinquents twice and even while incarcerated there, my black was a problem. An Indian girl there started calling me Cochise and that nickname has stuck with me ever since, but once I learned who Cochise really was, it was befitting for me as well, because I was wild and even crazy but very crafty to speak. Cochise was like an alter personality and she was a warrior, full of fire and she kept me in trouble, but she was also my defense. Cochise spoke bravely and was quick to fight but she was intelligent and crafty instigating endless problems with the law and at school and with my mother for sure. The last time I was there at the training school, a group of us girls had decided to escape with the ringleader, who was a white girl from Jackson, Mississippi. She instructed everyone what to do for she had stolen a knife and fork from our meal trays and my job was once they had apprehended the counselor on duty at knife point, I was to tie her up with torn bed sheets. I froze as the counselor was screaming so loudly, it freaked me out and I just stood there in utter fear and the counselor got away. They blamed me for the whole affair, sent the ringleader back to Jackson and put me in solitary confinement for two weeks, just me and a marbled slab and a naked black floor to sleep on. Soon I would run far away not knowing that I was trying to run away from myself and not just from my black condition but from life as I had come to know it.

Becoming Black almost cost me my life, but God had a plan for my good, even though I suffered great harm growing up, the impairments were growing lessons. Eventually I learned from my mistakes and later years revealed that I would suffer with enormous mental challenges. I didn't know what to do with myself, my emotions and anguish, and mom said she didn't know what to do with me either. Mother said I was born grown and never a child. She had no instructions on how to handle a teenager such as I had become and she just let me go, for she had others to provide for. Yet she never gave up on me but instead, she prayed for me. When I think of my teenage years, I too am appalled at my willingness to do things others my age wouldn't do. Fear was not a part of my character and I had the bravery of black bulls, not ever thinking of the dangers I was putting myself in. Being the youngest in my class, the Columbia High School Class of 1976, everything started early for me, being in high school at thirteen surrounded by a beautiful white people especially the white high school boys at Columbia High School was sheer delight. My best friend was a young white girl with long blonde hair, a sweetheart that I still adore to this day. Soon I realized that neither the white boys or the black boys had personal interests in me, but there were lots of older white boys outside the school that welcomed me and my sexual curiosities. They just wanted to explore, make tracks and hike through the black forest between my black thighs. My story is not of accusations, anger, or pointing fingers, nor is it about racism even though racism was the foundation for much of what I went through. This is mainly a story how I learned to overcome so many hindrances and how these teachings helped me to excel in life in due time. It seemed as if I was commanded to do whatever the whites asked me to but not live as they, but in what limited access given unto me. My mindset dictated that in order to get ahead in life, I had to go the white way and the white way was between my legs in that black forest of mine. Certainly, I knew also that many black women and girls got extra money from white men including the candy man who came by on Saturdays with his station wagon filled with ointments and bedspreads, to the insurance man and even the white man that came thru the neighborhood selling turnip, collard and mustard greens. It was hush-hush thing, but I was very aware and when those white men made it to me, I was so ready. I was determined to make my black work for me and I had to get mine. That black forest between my thighs was young, gifted and without shame, ready for exploration. It seems today the entrance to my black forest has been closed until further notice as I have given God the key. My young black was lame and untamed but my black was beautiful, although it had become very ugly.

Becoming Black was explosive and by the time I was fourteen, I was bad to the bone, finer than wine, pretty as hell, crazy as hell, but very intelligent and smart; at least that was what I thought. School was easy, as I didn't have to do a lot of studying and was a soon a superintendent scholar, but school was also problematic because I didn't know how to get in nor how to fit in. It would be many years later that I would be diagnosed with a dissociative identity disorder as I had no idea who I was and was easily influenced with no one to pattern myself after. It's also no wonder that I would one day have a mood disorder, borderline personality disorder, suffer with major depression, drug abuse, alcohol abuse, and a post-traumatic stress disorder. The groundwork had already been laid for the battles to come. Truly, I felt that I was already a woman having started by menstrual at the age of ten and already damaged in every dynamic of my being with no true vision of what I was supposed to be. There weren't any blacks in town I wanted to be like and the upper crust blacks with nice homes and education a few as there were, I didn't want to be like them either. It felt they looked down on my siblings and I, and I could feel the distaste as they looked down on my mother. Who was I but a young black girl with no voice and damaged, having never being a virgin and born guilty, who was I and how was I to become black.

Becoming Black revealed to me that I was low on the totem poles of life and an outcast to speak, yet I had something to prove. School was challenging and I got expelled a few times, and my mother who never gave up on me enrolled me at Prentiss Institute and there I was a fourteen-year-old teenager, surrounded by high school seniors and college freshmen and they too were black. Fate would have it that I was expelled from this school too as I forgot to sign out when leaving campus one weekend. It was said had I completed school there, I would have been one of the youngest high school graduates in the state of Mississippi and I felt my dismissal was navigated, and another form of hating. Yet I had to learn the black way no matter how oppressing it seemed to be. I was determined to get covered in white love and to marry me a white man, but soon I spiraled head first into a corrupt world of sex, drugs and dirty money. I was unaware that some of these experiences and explorations, would make changes in my life that I would one day regret and be ashamed of. I laugh today thinking about how Cosmopolitan Magazine groomed me to supposedly become more beautiful and attractive. I even wore fake nails and eyelashes when my siblings and I went to pick cucumbers and pull tomato plants to help momma with money before I was black. Picking cotton was pitiful and I didn't fare very well, so mom found other work for me in other produce fields. Already I knew I couldn't work no fields, clean no kitchens, wash and iron white laundry and certainly not work in any factory as I had already tried it. The only thing that seemed to work for me to acquire good money was my body, my black forest and my good looks. There were few black sexual engagements while becoming black, as I had no interest in a future with a black man. It was obvious as well that the white guys I slept with, did not want me as a wife and more so, didn't want others to know they were making trails in my black forest. Soon I was introduced to a different kind of white men with big money and businesses, who loved young black girls or shall I say who loved hiking in young fertile black forests. I had what they wanted and plenty of it and I was willing, because I wanted the white men with great money, as it seemed to be the best way. Before long, I had white undercover boyfriends, hikers and tricks at almost every business on the highway, and already I wasn't nothing less than a young black whore. Most of the whites I engaged had plenty of drugs and once in high school, I tried everything they offered to me regrettably. We had a long walk to school as my neighborhood had only one bus and it was privately owned and cost a quarter to ride. The bus was called Tic-Tac 42 and it leaked when it rained, but it was better than walking miles in the rain to school. Walking to school proved fruitful too as I met many white men while walking, that wanted to visit and take shelter in my black forest. Times were still far better than when we lived on that old black river bank, yet the struggle was real and yet quite oppressive for we had yet to overcome. On occasion, walking to and from school, white men would drive or pull up on us teenagers walking home from school, with their penis in their hands, grinning like they were doing us a favor. They have a word for men who do that kind of thing today and it's a crime that carries jail time. Unlike before, when it was done without remorse or consequences. I am so very thankful that those days are long gone and people everywhere are being held accountable for their wicked actions. In some areas we walked, we had to run like hell, past those "no niggers' neighborhoods to get away from white boys chasing us. We were taught to look out for one another and the whole neighborhood was family and even classmates. My mother taught her children how to fight, though it is frowned upon in today's world, we had to fight from time to time, get beaten up, raped or possibly die. I was already dead. Black was killing me. My experimentations with white men and their drugs led me into a downhill spiral which took many years to endure the consequences and overcome future addictions. No one told me that drug usage was supposed to be for recreational purposes, but instead, it was a prophesy of many black roads I was to later navigate and travel because of addictions. This thief in the night was black and had me in its sight.

Becoming Black encouraged and in return, quenched my thirst to be more than just black. My first loves were white and I alienated the black community and did everything with my new white friends. It was a most difficult time, being I didn't want to be black in the first place, yet I had to find something black within me. I was surrounded by a new white, a white that I wanted and most curious to explore. The desegregation of the schools was an introduction to a whole new lifestyle and culture specifically white Dirty South Mississippi culture, yet it was so exciting and new-fangled with various meandering crooked roads to further partake. These roads were harsh, as I had been discarded by black friends and neighbors and declared as a honky lover and I had to fight because of my affinity for whites. Being jumped on and getting whippings did not deter me from pursuing this precarious white thing. It wasn't that I wanted to be white but I desired that better quality of life they had and I wanted a bright future with prosperity and I was willing to pay for it, no matter the cost. Most whites I frequent with, had very nice homes, money, cars, marijuana and all sorts of drugs to include acid, liquid speed, crank, mushrooms, and those dirty needles. They had liquors, camp houses, tequila, lemon and salt as we went skinny dipping at midnight sometimes, at the gravel pits where I almost drowned trying to be white. The reason I was in the middle of a gravel pit hanging on to an inner tube and drunk in the middle of the night escapes me. I can't swim a lick and shouldn't have been in those black waters, but God is good as when I got snatched off the inner tube and I went down, down, down, He was there with me. Some folks would laugh at me as I would bath my caramel skin with suntan lotion because when I came out of the sun and took off my swimsuit, I had prominent tan lines which make me almost white. Silly me. One of my sisters told me recently that she and another sister of mine would laugh at me putting on suntan lotion to get darker while they were using Noxzema to lighten their skin. I would disappear for weeks at a time hanging out at my white friends' houses and I was welcomed there, sat down and ate with them and I never wanted to go back black or go back home, but I had to as I wasn't old enough to make such decisions. The same girl that saved my life at the gravel pits that night is the same one I ran away with in the middle of the night bound for Miami, Florida for some reason. We were making the great escape and headed out of Columbia in the middle of the night heading to Shreveport, Louisiana enroute to Miami where I thought I wanted to go, but we changed our minds and decided to go to Los Angeles instead and that's exactly where we headed with a few clothing and $11.40 in our pockets. Truckdrivers could pick up hitchhikers then and that was a blessing for us. Four days later, we were in the heart of Los Angeles, young dumb, curious and troubled and I'm sure we looked like fresh meat. We were quite a sight to behold with ebony and ivory on the road to somewhere, yet to nowhere.

 Becoming Black was a journey of great aspiration but consistently filled with confusion, great trial and errors, with all new engagements and perspectives exploding all around. It was not easy as I had learned at a young age that black was not the thing to be, even though I had absolutely nothing to do with it. The adventure to Los Angeles was remarkable and extremely adventurous, as I got to be a part of a culture that was greatly more than black. The stop in Shreveport, left us without any clothing as we slept and spent the nights with soldiers at Bossier City Air

Force Base nearby. In the day time we visited a black area nearby where many prostitutes lived and they stole all our belongings and we decided to go on toward California. The radio constantly played James Brown singing say it out loud, I'm black and I'm proud; while being black was becoming more attractive and desirable. Maybe black was something I could profit from, and something I could use to elevate in life. Maybe it was something that could set me free from that old black river and all them black folks surrounding me who did not have my best interest at heart. Maybe black was becoming a safe haven for me after all. Fourteen was an age of reckoning I thought, because I had new freedoms but had to engage the intelligence and bright mind I was born with. Being determined as I was, offered great support to my quest to be something other than black. Hitchhiking to Los Angeles challenged my mindset and once we were there, standing on the corner of the Avenue of Stars, we felt we had escaped the Dirty South, yet we were completely lost, but we made it and made it safely. A black man in a white van pulled up to us and said y'all look lost, let me take you somewhere you can meet people. He drove us to Santa Monica Beach and dropped us off. The beaches were splendid and refreshing, filled with all kinds of people with all kinds of skin tones and hair and it was absolutely breathtaking. Ironically, my girlfriend faced some of the stuff I faced in Mississippi in that a group of black guys came upon us, cursed her out calling her names, and told me I shouldn't be hanging out with a white girl, but soon we separated as she left with some white guy she met and I was all alone, on my own in The City of Angels. I wasn't afraid though, but very hesitant and skeptical of my newfound surroundings. Some gay guys befriended me and offered me a place to stay if I couldn't find some place to go. I stayed with them a few nights, while hanging out on the beach during the day. A young blue-eyed white gangster invited me to come stay with him in Hollywood and I did. He was seasoned and charismatic, groomed in black culture and language and he had smooth moves as he was a drug dealer. The next thing I knew, I was hooked on heroin with tracks running up and down my arms and ankles, and I was in grave danger. Looking back at these adventures only confirm that God has been watching over me since birth. The enemy had a plot for my demise but God had a plan for my future and He gave me hope. I had been hoping for something better since birth but now I was in big trouble. This white gangster from the beach left me at his apartment during the day and when he returned, he would accuse me of shooting up while he gone and he was so angry that he would shoot syringes full of heroin, in my face and eyes, slam me against the wall and choke me. The look in his eyes was pure rage coupled with heroin and he was also out of his mind. One evening before this wake-up call, he and I were both high as kites, nodding in and out on the mattress on the living room floor, when a guy just walked in and took all of his stash and money off the table and we couldn't respond, as all we could do was look at him, unable to move. More proof that I had to move on and I didn't know what to do or where else to go but I knew I had to get away from there. Many of the tenants in that complex he lived in were gay and they took a liking to me and I liked them because I was new to the gay life and drag queens and found it to be most curious but also thrilling. Cosmopolitan had taught me a lot with makeup application, plus I had mad skills being an artist and they would let me apply their make up and do their hair for various queen pageants and shows. Hollywood was gay and my gay friends had rich friends with mansions in Laurel Canyon and on Mulholland Drive. I loved being with them but one particular party we went to changed my mind because I was not the one any of those beautiful men wanted. One man I met was a Kickapoo Indian of Mexican descent and he was so gorgeous with locks of long curly black hair and pearly white teeth. His hair was so thick and wavy, he would take marijuana joints at parties and just tuck them in his hair where they remained until he shook them out. I simply adored him and I wanted him to visit my black forest and hike for a while. We went to a back bedroom to make out and while in bed, another man climbed in bed with us and they started making out as if I wasn't there anymore, and this turned me completely off. Yet I continued with my gay friends as I had no one else, and we would frequent almost every night, the Paradise Ballroom and The Other Side discotheques which both had grand strobe light dance floors. We would party all night, or just walk and shine up and down Hollywood Boulevard and the infamous Sunset Strip. It was unlike anything I ever imagined as I walked those streets many nights and made good money, but when I look at shows like Forensic Files, I know I was blessed not to have become a victim of death, as serial killers were on the prowl for girls like me. On one particular night, as I headed downtown to work the streets, I jumped into the wrong truck. When I got inside the truck, the driver a young white male made a U-turn and headed back toward Mount Lee where the famous Hollywood sign is and there at the base of the mountain, he stopped and two other white guys jumped in the truck trapping me in the middle, and up the mountain we went. The three of them tried to rape me but I was a fighter and had been studying kung fu thru the mail and I did a jump kick to one their faces and blood went everywhere. It scared them to the point that they took me back down the mountain and kicked me out. That jump kick saved my life because they probably would have killed me after they were done raping me and left me on top of that mountain, was my thought. I called the police and was all tattered and torn looking like a giant dust ball with my pants all ripped and hanging off, but the policeman said to just be thankful I was alive and I was. This didn't deter me as my youth had great confidence and I don't believe the color of my skin had anything to do with all of this but I was always the only young black girl involved. My gay friends invited me to go with them to a pre-concert party for the O'Jays one night, and while I was there, someone spiked my drink and I was awakened three days later by police on the other side of town.

    They found me between garbage cans behind a restaurant on Van Nuys Street. I had not been raped nor robbed as my hands and neck were still draped in turquoise which was popular then, but I had been thrown out like garbage, for dead. They kept me in the infirmary until my head cleared as I also had cold turkey from heroin then they released me and I never did heroin again thank God. Some of the gay guys I had met before took me to stay with a transvestite called Mother Trish and she was beyond my comprehension. She was from Sweden and before her transformation, she was John. and she took care of me, as God was still watching over me. I knew nothing about drag queens and had never been around them but I was amazed with the whole concept and some of the queens I met were the most beautiful with flawless makeup, and silicone injected boobs and hips. There I was living in the gay world and it was amusing. They would pay me with clothing and money to make up their faces and style their hair getting them ready for various pageants and shows and I was good at it. These are not stories I have conjured up as I have a police rap sheet a mile long that can testify most of my journey. Again, I was walking the streets of Hollywood every night making money with my body and this caused me to get arrested and go to jail for prostitution. With the fake information I gave the arresting policemen, I was arrested as Shelia Watts, twenty-four years old, booked into Sybil Brand Institute for Women and I was totally, out of my league. A Spanish woman was put in the holding tank where I was held and she had been arrested for possession of a huge amount of heroin and she had stashed some between her legs in her privates which she started handing out to us to get rid of it. I took a bag of what was called a speedball, a combination of heroin and cocaine and I snorted some of it, and it had everyone throwing up but we were flying high afterwards, in jail and I decided to keep some for later. This was a grave mistake as they searched everyone again and they found my little stash. I then had not only a prostitution charge but another charge for heroin possession and was facing up to ten years. I started crying like a baby and was ready to return home to my mother in Columbia when I told them the truth, that I was Dorothy Bee Jones and only fifteen years old. The judge requested a certified birth certificate from Mississippi and days later, I found myself being shipped to Los Padrinos Juvenile Hall in Downey, California. Los Padrinos was a peculiar and quaint little place with peacocks walking freely about and it had mostly a Chicano population, but soon I was on a plane with a police escort, though not in uniform, on my way home back to Mississippi. None of my experience in Los Angeles reflected any racism and had nothing to do with the color of my skin, yet I could be wrong because I certainly stood out. Now I already had the propensity to do drugs, make bad decisions and get in trouble with the law. All these memories are a testament to the goodness of God and serve as witness to my growth in self-discovery and the ideology of being black. Help me Lord as I journey into my own blackness.

Becoming Black meant returning to the place and the people I detested most, by way of to Pinebelt Regional Airport where a deputy from Marion County was waiting for me. With a huge teddy bear in my arms that the escort gave me at the LA International Airport, the deputy took it away from me as he handcuffed me getting off the airplane. I was just fifteen and I wasn't violent but I was still black and was treated like a hardened criminal being placed in jail with adult criminals once again, until the paperwork was completed in order for me go back home to my mother.

I had been smart while in juvenile hall at Los Padrinos, and had written a letter to the local judge, asking for forgiveness and to the pastor of my home church asking him to speak on my behalf that I not be locked up again like a caged animal. I was good with words as I read many books and the dictionary was still my good friend and I was very convincing and chose my words wisely. It worked and the courts gave me another chance to return back home with my mother and ironically, I was glad to be there. This was certainly a black thing as the only crime I had committed was to run away from home in the first place. Soon mother had again enrolled me back into Columbia High School and for a while, everything went smooth. The school yard had a smoking area with a huge tree behind the band hall where we would sit in a circle around it, smoke weed, sneak off, play hooky as I went to the homes of white friends where we drank good liquor. It was still my desire to marry a white man and live happily ever after.

Becoming Black forced me to face the truth, that none of the white men I had been sleeping with for money would ever love me or marry me. My thoughts that the key to love and marriage was buried in my black forest were a delusion as it became clear that I had no idea what love was or what a good man for marriage looked like. Two of those men, I was crazy about with one having just been released from prison and the other a respected local business man. The businessman was married yet I honestly believed he felt something for me as he spent a lot of time with me and he kept my wallet fat. He would send for me when out of town and took me with him to his cottages and camp houses even out of state in Alabama. This same man that I thought I was in love with, would one day rape me while I was on my cycle and lodged a tampon deep in my body, yet I told no one because I wasn't supposed to be at his house in the first place. I shouldered this blame for countless year as the assault had also unknowingly taken away my ability to bear children. I shouldn't have gone to him when he called, yet I thought he cared for me and I blamed myself for being in that situation. I became very ill a couple of weeks later and passed out one day in the living room at home for then I had Toxic Shock Syndrome, a result of pelvic inflammatory disease from the infection the tampon caused in my body. This traumatized my reproductive organs and is the very reason I don't have children today because of the scar tissue the infection left. At the time, I didn't know I would never be able to bear children, as that knowledge came many years later, yet I continued to be with this man for many years. I wanted children badly and felt less of a woman even though I was still a teenager, but all my classmates, neighbors and even my sisters were having babies. I wanted babies too and is my greatest regret today, the fact that I never birthed any children of my own. Even to this very day I blame myself as it is my philosophy that I put myself in these situations therefore I was to blame. Many layers of my injured psyche would have to be sorted through before I would become black and with purpose. It was not my purpose to marry and live happily after with a house full of children and grandchildren and most definitely it was not my purpose to marry a white man. Children are a precious gift from God and it is imperative they be given the proper material and nourishment in order to grow and become fruitful. Though I have no children of my own, I have learned through my own experiences growing up, what doesn't work for a healthy mentality and character. It took a myriad of counseling and therapy sessions to reiterate to me that I was not the blame for the many offenses made upon me, but I beg to differ, yet there is no guilt and no shame with my declaration. It is what it is and what it is, is just another shade of black.

Becoming Black forced me to reconsider my attendance in public schools as I was under attack not only by some neighbors but by a classmate as well. At school during lunchbreak a black classmate and a supposed friend, called me a honky lover, splashed a carton of white milk on me and assaulted me. My older sister walked into the lunchroom and saw him on top of me with a fork in his hand when she leaped to my rescue and we whipped his behind, together. My sister always showed up at the right time as many others tried to harm me and beat me up for being who I was trying to be. We both were expelled from school even though the principal congratulated us for whipping the guy like we did as he was a well-known bully. Now how black is that. We were yet in the middle of a strong racial divide and the lines were still clearly drawn. School was not going to work for me and I was done with it at fifteen, severely damaged and broken mentally, spiritually and physically but inside I kept my hope. Hope is a wonderful gift and it is that same hope my mother had as she told me that I was not going to lay around the house and do nothing as a school dropout. Most of the time, I babysit my sister's children and then momma gave birth to my youngest sister some twelve years after my baby brother. I named her and she was mine, yet, I had to find more to do and momma repeatedly said so. When I was younger watching that little black and white television we had, a commercial would come on with women in the armed forces stepping out one by one and saluting the flag. I loved that commercial not knowing that one day I too would join the military and salute that same flag. My mother took me to Gulfport Community College to take my GED test which I passed with flying colors and received my diploma along the same time my classmates graduated from high school. It was now 1976, and I was now seventeen years old enlisting in the US Army with my mother's approval as she signed that dotted line, and I was again on my way out of Columbia, out of Mississippi. I almost maxed the Army entrance test and the recruiters were aware that I had previous troubles at home and with the law, but they took me in because I was most intelligent with great potentials. My mother helped my older sister and I train for Basic Training as my older sister enlisted a month after myself and we were both joining the Women Army Corp (WAC). My mother would have us jog back and forth to Duckworth Park down the street from where we lived and she would have us to exercise daily. Mom wanted us both to be successful and to be somebody and I eternally thank her for this faith and encouragement. My sister and I were enlisted into the last command of the WACs as we were called, whereas the next year, the Corp was dismantled, and we became Army soldiers. It was one of my greatest accomplishments even though I didn't know at that time, it would lay the groundwork and financial stability for my success in my senior years. Maybe black wasn't so bad after all.

Becoming Black was beginning to look better for me and so much more promising as I went to Anniston, Alabama, for basic training and the people there were from all over the world, but had joined together for the sake of our country. It was a great feeling with men and women from every race to look upon, but basic training at Ft. McClelland was hard. I was a pretty girl and didn't care for crawling around in the mud and jumping over various obstacles including one particular tall wooden wall that I was never able to climb over. It felt horrible as I was an achiever and very competitive but that wall defeated me every time. The drill sergeant stood in my face screaming to me that I was sorry and my whole family was sorry, and all I could yell back, was yes sir drill sergeant! Weapons training, my M16, and defensive hand to hand combat tactics was my favorite part of back training and I was so proud to be in the Army as it turned out to be seemingly, a good thing for me. Yet, I barely completed basic training as I didn't like running long distances and twelve-mile night marches with full army gear, my weapon and Alice packs, but it was only by the grace of God, I finished it. The fact that I completed my training embraces one of my favorite verses in Jeremiah 29:11 in which God said He had a plan for me, for my good with hope and a future. While in basic training, I met a young handsome white military police trainee from New York and I fell head over heels in love. The freedom to date anyone on the military base reminded me of the interracial freedoms I witnessed in California, yet I was an enlisted soldier and could not fraternize but it did not stop me from trying of course. This was not a problem as the young trainee I dated, was also enlisted, and he was striking, standing over six feet tall, broad shoulders, with a smile as bright as the noon day sun. My rebel curiosity and spirit would take over soon, as I became good friends with another enlisted curly carrot top friend from California. She and I would sneak out the windows after bed check going to the 123 Club for enlisted soldiers. She was very high spirited, funny and she was like me, very adventurous. We snuck out every chance we got and I would meet my new love and everyone had a great time at this club drinking, dancing and partying. Soon, I decided to have sex with him and went with him to an abandoned barrack on the backside of the post and my life would never be the same. This story is my memoir to speak, and it documents how we can prevail, no matter how many obstacles and challenges come upon us in any given format. My curiosity and faulty ambitions triggered great turmoil and pain in my young life but they also obliged me with some of the best lessons in life. It was a huge mistake to think that this image of male pulchritude was in love with me as I thought he was, and I believed he wanted to marry me. We took so many pictures together, with me sitting on his lap and him with his arms around me looking so happy but I have long lost those pictures but not the memories as he made me happy and he looked very happy with me as well. Once we made it to the door of the abandoned barrack and I stepped inside, war broke out and I was attacked by several male enlistees. I recall fighting for my life and my last memory that night was the fight and going down hard. I don't know what all happened after that as I was either knocked out or hit my head when they slammed me to the floor. Years later while in therapy after a PTSD diagnosis for military sexual trauma, I was told by a counselor that God would not put more on me than I could bear and this had to be true because I don't even remember how I got back to my barracks nor do I remember the sexual violence against me and I thank God for this. When the doctors removed a six-centimeter brain tumor from my brain in 2015, many of my memories had left me but some memories would never delete and this memory of this assault proved to be fundamental to years of self-medication, drug abuse, self-abuse and alcoholism. Sharing my story has also awakened tremendous memory and though much is quite pained, I am thankful because entangled with the unpleasant memories are lovely and happy memories as well. Fortunately, I was resilient and bounced right back on track, not knowing that my mind had buried and would keep buried, the assault for a multitude of years, yet my doctors called it a special gift of mine from Almighty God. The doctors said I had the ability and gift to leave my body mentally when under trauma experiences. This gift has remained though there is no trauma in my life today. The last time my friend and I snuck out the windows to the club, we were busted by our drill sergeants and faced dismissal from basic training, but it was a few days before graduation and they let us progress and graduate. My commanding officer said he would forward a letter of this incident to my new CO at Ft. Jackson, South Carolina, where I went for Advanced Individual Training (AIT), but fortunately for me, my new CO said it had nothing to do with him but to not try that kind of thing with him and that was the end of that. Maybe black was not so bad after all and I became hopeful for new black life again.

    Becoming Black was still a distaste in my mouth and I still wanted to marry a white man and live the prosperous white life. Even with all the assaults against me by white males, it didn't discourage my quest for true white love. Though I had been sexually assaulted by black men in the past, it only confirmed my distaste for them yet it amplified my desire for marriage to a white man. AIT training was eventless but coed which was now the standard for the Army, as it involved military clerical training, drill and ceremonies and of course, lots of partying after training hours.

I soon graduated from AIT and went to my first permanent duty station at Ft. Ord in Monterey, California. I had found my way back to the state I loved most thus far and it was still amazing. When our bus pulled up to Ft. Ord, enlistees were sitting out on benches, drinking, smoking weed and playing loud music and it seemed the place to be. Now I was eighteen with a bullet and I felt right in place at Ft. Ord. While standing in line for chow at the mess hall one day, a man behind me said to me that I had a nice tush. I thanked him and we introduced ourselves and the quest for white love was on once again. One would think I had learned my lesson but I had more clarity now and made better choices with the white men. He and I began dating and he was unlike any white man I had ever met as he was Polish, from Pawtucket, Rhode Island, with a slight accent and ever so, a gentleman. Just imagine a twenty-four-year- old half bald Polish man with silver sideburns and myself a beautiful young eighteen-year-old black girl from the Dirty South, and yes, he was white enough for me. After months of dating, he proposed to me even though his parents were against it and my mother was furious when I told her about it, after sending her professional photos we had taken together. We continued our love affair as he was a man of high culture and education and he was an emergency room technician. He took me everywhere in Monterey Seaside, to wine and cheese tasting programs, introducing me to a finer lifestyle as I became a connoisseur of fine wines while he educated in high culture. He seized every moment he could with me as we visited and toured southern California, inclusive of Big Sur, Fisherman Wharf in San Francisco, Cannery Row, San Jose Boardwalk and El Toro Park in Salinas. My favorite places were the San Francisco Zoo with the Japanese Tea Garden, and Marriotts Great America, which exposed me to the various dynamics of different lifestyles and cultures unknown to me. We went to pumpkin festivals and drank wine at Carmel by the Sea gazing upon the Lone Cypress, and on lazy days we strolled on Pebble Beach and I simply loved everything he introduced me to and was in awe of the many places he loved taking me. For my nineteenth birthday, this attractive young Polish man charmed me with a private birthday party at Ye Old Bathhouse in Pacific Grove. It was grand as some of the dining area and dance floor was glass with the ocean splashing on the rocks below. It was a sight to behold and it was a good space to be in, especially for that time and place in our society as I finally began to feel like I belonged somewhere and already had enough good memories to last a lifetime. California was spectacular and provided great educations of how different cultures lived and engaged each other without restraints and seemingly without racism. It appeared that my life wasn't so black after all with white linings lingering on the horizon, with no black clouds in sight.

Becoming Black mirrored a voyage of relentless change and as fate would have it, a unsettling change was headed my way that would affect and neglect my current love affair as I got orders to go to Germany. It was not my desire to go to Europe and I couldn't get out of it as it didn't matter to the military that I was in love with a Polish man who wanted to marry me. The trip to Germany was exciting, flying high above the horizon in a C-140 cargo plane full of male enlistees bursting with laughter and hidden fears. Soon enough, I would fall in love with the country but my first assignment was in Grafenwoehr, West Germany on the southern boundary and it was deplorable. The barracks were very old, damp and cold with German and Dutch soldiers on both sides who drank beer all the time. In order to get heat, we had to go outside, pump oil into a metal can, climb back up three flights of stairs, pour the oil into the furnace and light it, only to watch everything get covered in black soot. It was a training camp where I spent countless hours in the woods on field maneuvers and I was miserable, missing my Polish man back at Ft. Ord. Fortunately, I was reassigned and stationed off the North Sea at Clay Kaserne in Osterholz-Scharmbeck situated between Bremen and Bremerhaven while it was still in construction. Serving as an Administrative Specialist Four working for Headquarters, Headquarters Command with the 2ndArmored "Hell on Wheels" Division (Forward), I was finally a somebody with a top secret and NATO top secret clearance. Military training maneuvers were unyielding and threatening as I found myself again in the blackness of night, in the black fields again, surrounded my uncountable black soldiers, deep in the ice-covered countryside, sleeping in a frozen pup tent, taking sponge baths with a helmet, and water heated from a sterno kit. Germany was brutally cold, and the heavy snow was unbearable forcing us to maneuver around the post in military tanks above the icy grounds. I was never lucky enough to be trapped off post when the snow blizzards arose. My canteen never ever had water in it, unlike the time I trained in the Mojave Desert on a joint task force mission when water was a absolute necessity but it only contained apple schnaps or some other kind of liquor in Europe. There were few women training with me in the barren cold fields of Germany and it made me uneasy but I never had another problem like I did in basic training. Alcohol was a good friend to my comrades and I, and we entertained ourselves after work hours, drinking and smoking heavy, jumping out of the third-floor windows into the snow, we didn't need refrigerators either, hanging our bagged food outside on the window handles. This mirrored the black capacity to make things work for us from nothing.

Becoming Black finally began to appeal to me as I met and became friends with other young black women assigned to my unit and that were ambitious, exciting, experienced, savvy, educated and they were city girls. They didn't work in kitchens and factories; they had dreams that I never dared to dream. It was a different kind of black people stationed in Europe, with many of them from the East Coast and places like Chicago and New York, and I learned a lot from these young black women, especially concerning fashion and lady-like behavior. They introduced to me the concept of style and class. Yet, I missed my man and though people say absence makes the heart grow fonder, it didn't for me, as my fiancé at Ft. Ord started dating someone else and that killed my romantic interests in him and our chances for marriage. Dating the white soldiers in Germany was different and repulsive, as they drank too much with no apparent focus. It was unclear to me why I surmised that marriage to a white man would afford me freedom, liberty and financial stability but changes to offset that frame of thought were soon underway. A new kind of black man all fine, well-dressed and dapper began to catch my attention as they wore London Fog trench coats, Stacy Adams shoes and hats, leathers and fur, three- piece suits and they began to charm me right off my feet, with some of them sporting elaborate walking sticks. This was the first time ever that I wanted to be black and to marry a black man. These men carried themselves differently with great pride and confidence, unlike the poor, broken down alcoholic black men of my youth and I was significantly impressed. The problem was that I didn't know what love looked like, or felt like and I certainly didn't know how to measure a good man but found myself just having sex. Sex was different also, as my Polish man had taught and shown me what an orgasm was and I regretted the numerous times I was just going through the motions, just happy that the man was satisfied. My black forest had a quite a few different trails in it but none of them had led to volcanic-like explosions such as I experienced with him. However, the black men I had relations with in Germany made it clear that their desire was to please me and that alone was absolutely pleasing to me. These high steppers were young black entrepreneurs and serving our country was just part of their master plan to greatness. They were all about making big money and becoming successful in life and when a particular group of five black guys approached me one night at an African Club called the Voom-Voom Room which I loved and went to quite often, as they really knew how to party over there with African and Jamaican men swathing the club. I really never knew just how beautiful black could be until I met the new black people in Europe. This group of men came upon me and we all sat down at a table and they asked me to work with them in a business they had already well established. It was a new adventure summoning me and I was totally on board. They said they had been watching me and wanted me to be a part of their business ventures. Immediately I thought they were talking our maybe stealing or robbing but quickly they made it clear they were not, as I had stolen a purse from a German woman, took her wallet out and took it to them. They freaked out and threw the wallet where it could be found, sat me down and discussed their business designs with me. I was so embarrassed and confused as it turned out their organization was about the purchase and distribution of marijuana on and off post within a fifty-mile radius. The next thing I knew, I was catching trains to Belgium, Amsterdam and Copenhagen purchasing weed and bringing it back on post to be broken down, packaged and delivered to runners they had already in place We would be up all night at times, packaging the marijuana that sat high on a table like a mountain and I was cool with it and had never seen blacks doing it at this level. Again, I was a somebody with a name and a purpose and I never thought about the legal dangers of it all nor did I ever think about being caught; I just did my job and was paid well for doing it. After purchasing the weed in various cities, I would then place it in a black satchel and tuck the satchel under a different seat than where I sat and I never had a problem doing so. Soon I had my own big money buying furs, London Fog, gold jewelry, top notch stereo equipment and the utmost leathers and yet, there were no prerequisites that led to a hike in that black forest of mine. The entrance to my black forest was wide open yet seeking true love. Europe was awesome as I explored its countryside, from Bremen to Munich to include Nuremberg, Frankfurt, Stuttgart and Wiesbaden and countless other places of interest, visiting spectacular castles like the ones in fairytales. The landscape was splendid, green and fertile, while riding ferries up and down the North Sea was just one big celebration with Octoberfest as the granddaddy of it all. Memories of my training in Grafenwoehr would soon fade and I never desired to go there again as it was near the border too and somewhat dangerous for US Soldiers. It was truly amazing and ironic to visit the nightlife in some areas only to be told that no American soldiers were allowed inside, but I don't think that was called racism, it was something else, as my comrades were from all over the world. The military in Germany sponsored several programs allowing soldiers to interact with the community providing me the opportunity to meet a widowed and kind German man who admired me profusely. Love was not on our agenda, but the friendship was remarkable as he invited me to spend Christmas 1978, with him and his family. It was an incredible and welcomed experience, yet it was original and intriguing culture, eating pickled herring and brotchen at midmorning and bratwurst and pommes frites in the afternoon with champagne. He trusted me with his alligator green Mercedes Benz and I thought I was the shit. My black had become beautiful and I didn't have to spread my legs so intently, to see it. German food was curious and there I were but a few dishes I liked, but I did like the Schnitzel and pommes frites, most of all, I liked being happy and black. Germany was most captivating and educational for me as I sampled the good life and was yet a soldier in the United States Army. There I was, a black female soldier trying to buy a preowned, antique yellow gold Jaguar XJ6, that was most seductive, to take back home with me, but couldn't afford the shipping cost back to the United States nor could I afford to have the emissions system upgraded to meet US standards. My application for an overseas out and to get discharged in Germany was denied as I had waited too late to apply for it. Europe will always hold a special place in my heart as it was there, I became black with anticipation to accept and love myself as a young black woman. My black had finally become beautiful.

Becoming Black commanded and demanded that I make an essential return to Mississippi, to the very place I had tried so desperately to get away from with all its' black oppression and despair. Not much had changed, but life was a bit better at home as mother had a new brick home having lost the other wooden house to fire. Some businesses and banks had token blacks working at the front desks and counters and it was grand. The oil industry had piloted a program to hire women to work offshore on the oil rigs and I got hired by Poole Offshore in Harvey, Louisiana which lasted no more than six months as I still didn't like getting dirty and even more so, I wasn't cut for manual labor. The slight affinity I still had for white men soon faded because I had been introduced to that good black man while in Germany and it was now my preference. Something was yet missing within myself and I didn't have a clue how to pick a good man in the Dirty South. Before long, I met a beautiful black man from Canton, MS whom I dated for over a year with hopes to marry until one day the tables turned again and I found myself in grave danger. While at mom's new house, a freak incident occurred that led this man to beat me extremely and severely, knocking me unconscious. My head was swollen twice it's normal size, both my eyes were shut and mom had to feed me with a straw and that was the end of this affair. My younger brother saved my life that day when he broke down the door to my bedroom when he heard me screaming, but by then I was lying unconscious on the floor with this man still sitting on top of me, punching me in the head. It was truly a design of the enemy as he and I were playing around when it felt like he punched me in the nose and I responded by picking up an ornament on the dresser and striking him with it. When he walked to the mirror and pulled a tooth out of his bottom lip, I knew I was in trouble and the look in his eyes told me to run. I tried to get away, but by the time I got my hand on the door knob, it was too late and it was the worst beating I ever suffered from a man. It seemed I was following the same patterns as I witnessed with my mother, getting into violent relationships and harboring within myself, violent tendencies. My siblings and I had been raised to fight back if assaulted and fight to win, but all fights cannot be won. I'm thankful that I survived that incident yet I was curious about my choice of men. Was it genetic or a learned behavior or was I just mimicking my environment was a question I had yet to find the answer to. Already in my youth, I had seen my mother assaulted, bleeding and knocked unconscious by her own husband and it clearly wasn't what I sought in my life. My concept of a good man was limited, uninformed and challenged. It was imperative I make better choices but I lacked the education therein. My quest to become black, enjoy being black, to marry a good black man and birth beautiful black children was yet, just a dream. Regrettably, I had nothing to define my black choices.

Becoming Black mandated the fulfilment of a higher level of education and experiences, and I enrolled and became a student in 1982, at Pearl River Community College which is now a university, to study Journalism. Math and science were not favorite subjects of mine and I chose a course of study that required the least hours in those two classes. Writing was natural for me as I always loved the dictionary, terminology, the usage of colorful, creative speech and writing, it was all still so exciting to me. Feeling educated and being educated were vastly two different fundamentals and again, I became an academic scholar with excellent grades. While in my freshman year, I met a fast talking, proud walking, and handsome man from Bay St. Louis who swept me off my feet. He was smart, tall and good looking, with his briefcase, white button-down shirt and tie and he was a pre-med student with enormous potentials for a husband. Three months later, we were married on my birthday New Year Day 1983 and it was one of the worst mistakes of my life as I didn't realize I was on the rebound from my last love affair. Within months, my new husband and I were fighting and he had no limitations as it appeared he wanted me dead or close to it, if he couldn't have me. Thinking about the three brain tumors I have today, cause me to wonder if they resulted from the numerous assaults to my head, mostly coming from people that I thought I loved. My story is not the cries of a victim and seeks not sympathy, but is the sharing of my meandering and difficult journey to victory. It is often said we are defined by the choices we make yet I argue choices come with background information and you can't choose positively if you don't understand the context of the choices. Had I known better, I would've chosen many paths with greater perspectives. My ghetto black education was limited and my exposure to what a good man or father is or isn't was not illustrated to me on those dusty gravel roads. The man I married was a shady choice for me, not saying he was bad, but the behaviors he showed me before marriage soon changed to something sinister, demeaning and unsafe; most certainly, it was not love. Yes, he was good looking, tall, and educated with dreams and hopes for the better, but he too, was a prime candidate for anger management. His own mother had to call the police on him for trespassing, when we stayed with her. He had cursed her out in her own kitchen and when the police arrived, my puppy, a miniature doberman pincher Lady, ran up to my husband and he punched her in the head so hard, it killed her immediately and the police took him straight to jail for trespassing and animal cruelty. It wasn't long before I too had to call the police on him when he opened up my head with my own stiletto heel pump after it came off my foot he held while dragging me down the street. For some awkward and crazy reason, I would allow him to woo me back into his arms, subjecting myself to further altercations and assaults. Ultimately, I became pregnant, but the damage my fallopian tubes incurred from the pelvic inflammatory disease I got after the rape when I was fourteen, was too great and the baby did not survive, as it was trapped in my tubes. It aborted itself during my third month of pregnancy and today, I know it was not meant to be and was not the will of God. Yet I remained with my new husband and found myself on another journey away from my home state, traveling to Omaha, Nebraska where he had found work with a distant cousin. It wasn't long before I was fighting for my life again, with another head injury but with a greater will to get away from this man I married and survive. The last time I called the police for help in Omaha, they told me to get me a couple of friends called Smith and Wesson and that's exactly what I did. I left my husband and found my own apartment, but we still talked occasionally by phone as I did not trust him and I had the tendency to take him back again and again. Nebraska had the same kind of winters, I braved in Germany and on one particular morning my husband called to see if my car would start, which it didn't, so he offered to come over and start it so I could get to work. He came over and when I opened the door to let him in, he turned and pushed me out the door, locking me out of my own place, in the cold. When he reopened the door, he came out running, and when I walked back inside, I realized he had stolen my wallet and all my money. This infuriated me as I walked to his house with my gun in my pocket, in the snow, but he was gone. I thank God he was gone because I know I would have shot or possibly killed him and later, I learned that he had taken my money and flew out to Los Angeles. This worked for me as I thought I was free of him and I found me another apartment and began working for the City of Omaha. Life was looking better again as I started as a seasonal clerk for the city but soon got the position of Administrative Secretary and Receptionist for the City of Omaha, City Clerk's Office. It was an exciting time in my life as I loved my job with the city and my part time job with Omaha Today Magazine where I was a staff writer and feature editor. Having studied astrology, I also wrote a horoscope column for City Slicker Magazine of Omaha and the money I was making was fabulous. I was stunting and fronting with my Norma Kamali and Bill Blass high fashions of the 80s, but Omaha was too cold for me with -40 temperatures during winter, and after three years, I moved back to Mississippi. On my return, I was completely black, shining in proud ebony, feeling royal and accomplished and it felt great. It was also a great honor on my return to be employed as the first black news reporter and staff writer for the Columbian Progress, our local newspaper in Columbia in the year 1986. Greatness was within me all along, yet I had many layers of self to uncover and many more rivers to cross to find the greatness I was made in the image of. One of the first stories I had to cover caused me great misfortune as I made the front page on many issues writing stories as an investigative reporter. A local white woman had been killed at her place of business, and it was being blamed on a good friend of mine in which I knew she didn't do it, because I was with her on that particular night. People were calling me from all over the state with information about the murder and I was happy to print the information given to me. I began to receive threatening phone calls and someone even called my mother telling her they were going to blow up her house. My dreams had also been most troubling at this point in time, and I pay close attention to my dreams just like my mother did, because sometimes they are a premonition. Dreams and visions are a gift from God and my dreams compelled me to believe I was in grave danger concerning my work with the newspaper story. One dream in particular involved my brand-new candy apple red Cavalier I bought in Omaha, sinking down head first, in that old snaky black Pearl River. This didn't deter my ambition and drive to become a top-notch reporter, until one morning in the office, someone called and said to me that I had screwed up and should've kept quiet, that I had fucked up is what they said, and that scared me to death. Not long thereafter, on the same morning, I received another phone call which took the wind out of my very soul. This call was from a man in Los Angeles that said he wanted to marry my husband and that he needed me to divorce my husband so he could then marry him. He told me that if I didn't divorce him, that his mother was an attorney and together with my husband, they would sue me for a divorce and I would have to pay alimony. This black cloud that I was born under was thunderous now and the lightening had struck and burned deep in my heart again. To learn that the man I married was living with a gay man and was himself now gay, was too much for me to bear and I completely lost it. Crying, heartbroken, and full of fear, I called my friend, the same one they were accusing of murdering that white woman, came to my rescue and took me to her home where I could pull myself back together. I kept thinking about the times my husband had beaten me, putting me in the hospital when he opened my head with a gin bottle and my own shoe, and to think that he was gay was unbearable. Recalling all the fun I had with my gay friends when I lived in Los Angeles before, turned sour and the tables had turned and it felt that maybe this new black ordeal was some sort of ugly black and unwanted destination. With no one to trust, not even at the newspaper, I had to get away again, life had again, become blackest. A couple of days later, I got in my Cavalier, with my Saturday night special, a 38 handgun, that I bought from the neighborhood pawn shop, and I headed to Los Angeles with the intent to kill the both of them. I drove to LA and found them at the apartment where they lived but the spirit of God intervened and I didn't kill them but I was curious to know how this came to be, so I approached them in peace and they invited me in. Soon, I learned from the mouth of my husband that he had been sleeping with men off and on, since he was fourteen. He said the first time he had an orgasm was from a man giving him head when he was a young boy and that he never forgot that explosive and powerful feeling. I was floored, but I knew I could not leave him there with that gay man who had called me and we left together. It was another huge mistake on my part, because my husband was smoking rock cocaine and introduced me to it, but it was only recreational for me at that time. My black story, is a small testament of truth and seeks the ear of anyone listening how black life can appear sometimes, but we keep moving our little black feet until they become black with greatness. Life has been filled with so many black lies and intentions but it was too late to turn back, I was moving forward still black and ever so proud. A big beautiful black woman looked me in the eyes of my mirrors and she was still smiling. Black feet don't fail me now.

Becoming Black presented itself as a dark fiction, a gritty, shady piece of literature with me as its' leading character and protagonist. It was all unreal as I had accepted the fact that I would not marry a white man and live that happily ever after fairytale, yet I was not content with my experiences with black men. In my own skin, I did not want to be anymore, however I was too young to give up, sit down and die, and I knew there had to be more than the life I'd lived thus far. The men in my past were not good selections and I had no idea what a good choice looked like. My existence, and my story was like that black cat, something to be avoided, but everything happening with me was very real and suffocating in haziness. This black cloud I felt I was born under was no longer black, it was now white, just like that hard white crack that I became seriously addicted to in the near future. Back to Mississippi I went yet again, where crack was rampant and ravishing the land as it seemed everyone was either smoking it or snorting it and I could not stay there long either. Experiences in my home state, were roughly black indeed, but it was the closest thing I had with a small measure of a safety net. Hometowns may be challenging but there is a safe place there, somewhere, and always. I had greatness to discover and I left Columbia once again and went to Dallas, Texas to stay with my uncle hoping to get my life back together. After living with my uncle a few months, I got my own place in North Dallas, on Forest Lane, because Oak Cliff where my uncle lived and South Dallas were both oppressive, dangerous and primarily black. The south areas were too much like what I was running from just in a greater capacity. There is a whole lot of black folks in South Dallas. It seemed there was something about me that attracted the ugliness in black men. While on my way to work one day, walking to the bus stop, a black man offered me a ride but soon we were at his house because he said he had forgotten something he need for his job. Once going inside against my better judgement, he attacked me and tried to rape me and he almost succeeded but I was a fighter and it was hard to take me down single handedly. I began snatching curtains down and knocking over everything as we fought, trying to get him off me and to leave evidence I had been there. Praise be to God, I managed to get away from him, run down the street and call the police on him. Fortunately for me, but not for him, I had bitten him seriously on his arm and wrist during his attack on me and when the police located him, they arrested him when they saw the fresh bite marks on him as I reported to them. The jobs in Dallas were plentiful and the pay scale was the top I had seen, maybe too great as I began to meet professional people with good jobs that smoked crack after work and on the weekends. The crack in Dallas was unlike any I had ever smoked, and its effect was vastly different than the rock cocaine I smoked in Los Angeles. The coke I smoked in Los Angeles, zoned in a vacant blankness and numbness without an immediate need or want for more unlike crack. No one was jumping up trying to get more, every one sat around in another space and time. Black and smokey. It was like being locked in an atmospheric time zone for hours and I like that much better than the chase of crack cocaine. Scottie kept you moving, hustling and bustling but this was lethargic and tense as we moved around like zombies. When I smoked rocks in Dallas, that first fresh hit felt like an explosive orgasm to the point I would go to the bathroom to check between my legs. It was just an out of this world sensation, almost volcanic and quickly, I became addicted and hungry for it, even though I didn't know what addiction was at that time. Maybe I was just naive and too trusting, but I soon learned that appearances are mostly a presentation and not everyone is what they present themselves to be. Men dressed in nice suits with awesome jobs as were many of the women I met, led a whole different lifestyle after work and in their homes. Truly I was very confused and soon I was driving to work on Northwest Highway with a crackpipe in my mouth even stopping at McDonald's along the way, going into their bathrooms to get me a hit. This new addiction to crack happened quickly with intent to take me under, and it led me down a dangerous, spiraling slope of self-destruction. Eventually, I was cracked out and on one of my last jobs, I got caught stealing and forging company checks, being sentenced to ten years in prison. Luckily the prisons were full and I served only four months before my release. My crack addiction was cruel and mean, desperate and exhausting; it was so bad, my dope fiend, that I walked the streets of North Dallas, sleeping on air conditioning units behind office buildings at night still chasing crack and was completely out of my mind. Everything about my actions were black because I would almost kill, certainly steal and destroy anything that kept me from feeding my addiction. The devil is not red with horns and a tail; this devil was white, crunchy and cracked. The only thing I had going for me was my beautiful face and body. Eventually I caught a ride with a gorgeous young black man headed to Miami and I was Miami bound as we took turns driving, but I never made it there. It's was the fourth of July, road blocks were everywhere on the highway near Santa Rosa, Florida. I was driving and stopped to hand trooper my license, when he said get out the car, put your hands behind your back, we have a felony warrant for your arrest from the state of Mississippi and we have arrest you and take you into our custody. Not only was the black cloud over my head getting darker and larger, but I was truly in the top ten on the blacklist of life. My life was a black plague and now I am on my way back to that damn Mississippi to the City of Charm on the River Pearl barely with my new black lungs. My lungs had to be black because I tried to smoke all the crack I could find in Dallas. It wasn't meant for me to go to Miami, as I had now tried twice to get there and I thank God for protecting me from my own self. Not only had black proven to be a great enemy, but I, the young black crackhead, was truly the greatest enemy of all and of myself. Ironically, I had just begun to like my black, it had hope.

    Becoming Black had greater and more complicated lessons in this Black 101 class I had yet to learn, in my home state that I was unaware of, afraid of and yet most curious of. Sometimes moving forward requires stepping backwards a place or two. I thought I was moving forward in Dallas, but I wasn't because I was free ironically, and in jail at the same time. Now I'm being extradited back to Mississippi from Santa Rosa jail with a felony warrant for sales and possession of a controlled substance to wit cocaine. Within a couple of weeks, law officials from Columbia, Marion County came and got me as we headed back, little black me on that black back seat, handcuffed, as they, the two white police people, only uncuffed me to eat and go to the restroom. I don't know who or what I felt like but I knew one thing for sure, I had never sold drugs because I like cocaine too much to sell it. What manner of evil is this! Two white uniform police or deputies are in the front seat with me caged in the back seat and no one is talking to me. I was either going home to be with my Lord or to a home and without any doubt, a place I didn't belong. That black ass Mississippi with that long black ass river was out to swallow my black ass up again. Forget about being black, I was dead, these white folks are going to kill me along the way somewhere and throw me in them black woods on both side of the highway. The language of my story is a language of old, rich in my hood black culture, but communication is the key, less we forget. I've been black all along because my culture is heavy in my DNA and I have and will use some colorful expressions at time. My black was creative before I was black and still is, becoming black. I am not black yet, but journey with me as I try to become black because black don't crack and it's for sure that white isn't right. On the way back to Columbia, I spent the night at Mobile jail before we continued on and it was the most horrible jail I've encountered and needs no more review. Sleep was not on the agenda for me with my mind racing not knowing what the arrest and extradition was about. White folks were still killing black folks burying them in shallow graves and such, but I knew a God that had a plan for me and I prayed, prayed, and prayed even more. The female tank at Marion County jail was crammed with no place to lay down and it was jam-packed with my black sisters from all over town and every walk of life. When I saw my friends, as they all were, I was consumed with fear and knew something great and devastating was amidst. After talking with them, I glimpsed the truth of how my new black truth had locked me behinds those rusty black cell bars with me now sleeping on that damp cold black concrete floor. A few of the ladies spoke about a man that came to their homes with a so-called friend to purchase drugs. When they said he looked like a Cajun, I immediately recalled the night a friend called me and said his friend from New Orleans was in town and they wanted to party, asking me if I wanted to go with them. That man was a federal undercover narcotics agent and my friend was working with them to incriminate as many people as possible in the drug business. They picked me up and we rode around specifically on Owens Street in Columbia which had clubs up and down the street. Then this man asked me if I knew where to get some snow, some cocaine and of course that was right up my alley. He put $120 in my hand and I flagged a dealer passing by, who then pulled up beside us and I handed him the money and he handed me the cocaine which I handed over to the guy and that's how I got a sales charge. It truly was entrapment yet I got seven years in prison for my participation. The law came to my house to get me and provoke me to break the law so they could ruin my future in Mississippi with this first felony drug conviction. This is the moment, I became black and equal to all my other black sisters and brothers in jail at this same time, having been victimized by the same police system that was supposed to protect and serve. Facing thirty years in prison, I took the plea deal they offered me, whereas they dropped the sales charge and offered me the seven years for possession. What else could I do with no monies for a good lawyer and no way out because I was truly entrapped and black. Now I needed some black magic to eliminate my black prison sentence.

Becoming Black landed me in prison where I completed a three- and-a-half-year sentence flat time at Rankin County Correctional Facility where most of the inmates were black, oppressed and distressed. While in prison, I knew that I could not ever return to prison for any reason as there's nothing better than freedom. Prison was hard and I had no real support but my mother did her best to come see me and send money when she could. Fortunately, I became friends with a young woman who felt like she was a man, who then approached me to be her girlfriend. We were now a couple and she supported me greatly. I explored this relationship as much as I was able to, but I had and have no affinity for relations with another woman. It's not natural and it was combustive. The greatness already within me stepped to the forefront, as I went to the newly formed Cosmetology school there and got my Cosmetology license. I had been good at making people hair and faces more beautiful all my life thus far and graduated top of my class. Before long, I was styling officers' hair and designing sculptured nails and in return, I earned money and they brought me products to do my own upkeep. God created us all to shine and I was again shining, but in prison. The Cosmetology School had visitors in the industry from the free world come and speak with us and review our progress. One of the speakers owned a salon in Jackson and he told me that I could come work for him when I got my license and was released. Contacting him when I was free, landed me a job with one of the finest and most successful salons in Jackson, it being Tony's Hair and Nail Galleria where I crafted and perfected my skills and made respectable income. That good respectable money awakened my cocaine addiction, that sleeping tiger, and soon I was spiraling downhill again on the black path to self-destruction. I could write a whole different book about my experiences with crack addiction as it was the worse affliction of my life that I had to ultimately overcome. With more than fifteen recovery programs under my belt, from Mississippi to Arizona, I took good notes and I learned a lot about recovery but not the application of this knowledge to my life. Though crack is white, it became a black thang as it was introduced to black communities by a menacing white populace. Crack is white and not black, but black don't crack and black finds a way back.

    Becoming Black pierced my soul, as I learned no matter where you go, there you are and you can't run away from yourself. If I kept running in the circles I had been running, chasing myself, nothing would change, but if I paused just for a minute, stabilize myself with balance, I might glimpse who I really was or maybe who I was meant to be. Hindsight discloses that I had been running from me a very long time, as it wasn't just the black label I was running from. It wasn't until, I went to a program in Prescott, AZ at the VA hospital at Ft. Whipple that I gained a deeper view inside myself as they offered many different kinds of therapies and I flourished. Entering some of my artworks into the Arizona State Fair competition, winning blue ribbons, making quilts and painting rocks were just a few recovery tactics I embraced. After a year of residential treatment, living in the domiciliary, I was able to once again, get clean, get an apartment, get a job and gain recovery time. My employment as a licensed cosmetologist at J.C. Penny Spa Salon, Regis, and Master Cuts all provided me a firm foundation in the beauty industry specifically with Caucasian hair. I loved working in the salon and my repeat clientele were senior white ladies who loved to talk. It was refreshing and ironic as well, because I enjoyed it tremendously. There wasn't a large black population in Prescott and nearby communities which agreed with me because my black stood out now and was seemingly invited to become a part of the surroundings, if that makes sense. It was also there that I was diagnosed with PTSD and the many dynamics of it to include mood disorders, major depression, drug and alcohol abuse and it was a far cry from my original diagnosis of Multiple Personality Disorder while at the Jackson VA Medical Center. That diagnosis was soon exposed to be a dissociative identity disorder to which I truly qualified as I displayed all the symptoms especially the fugue state of being. Feelings of other girls living inside me, intrusive and dangerous thought patterns and living outside of myself, were all symptoms I dealt with daily. Feeling detached from my own body and mind as well as the world, was excessive for me and I was told by my psychiatrists on different occasions that no matter how uncomfortable it was, it was also a gift. The many times I was under assault or being raped, I was able to endure and possibly survive the stress of it all, was only because I could mentally leave my body, leave this world and find a safe place. I call it the grace of God that was upon me. So many times, I found myself in places not remembering how I got there even traveling to different cities and states. I would just pick myself up, dust myself off, and move on with the new environments not ever thinking I was under mental challenges and attacks. Determination was in my DNA and inherited from my mother, as today I can relate to the depression, I had seen upon her. Resilience is truly a black thing with all the oppression we had to overcome to discover our own greatness.

Becoming Black was an internal war within myself that I desired to overcome and learn to accept me for me, even though me was pretty black, me was not so beautiful yet. I longed to know who I truly was without all the ugly black adjectives. Ownership of my past was imperative because I too was partly responsible and contributed to the many battles I had to fight. My PTSD diagnosis ironically, gave me the help and guidance I needed to help remove and convert many of the ugly adjectives attached to me. It was now the time to get butt naked, let go of all the ugliness and make room for my God given internal beauty and greatness. In our superficial society, my outside was flawless, but my inside was black as tar. It didn't matter how the tar had seeped inside me but the result of it had to find a positive resolve and tolerance. Not only had I been diagnosed with PTSD, but with a bi-polar disorder as well, which can be a component of traumatic stress. Bi-polar issues are crazy as hell and I must have been bi-polar from birth with all the black dust grooming me. It's a blessing that we have mental health providers and programs that deliver results. Look at me today, I am not crazy after all. Many people including some family, called me crazy and I too thought I was crazy, doing things I didn't understand why, but I liked being crazy as it offered me a measure of identity. Just like with my crack addiction, it gave me purpose, no matter how destructive it was, it made me different. It was the thorn in my flesh, and it was an affliction I thought would die with. I even questioned if there were crazy crackhead people in heaven, because heaven was already mine as I truly believed in God, I was just broken and damaged. Dissociation I learned, stemmed mostly from a history of trauma and abuse, coupled with my unforgiving, yet promising black label. When I think about the times, I wanted to blow up my old neighborhood starting with my mother's house, I am so thankful to God and to the Department of Veteran Affairs. God gave me discernment that I needed help, courage to seek that help, strength to ask for it and endurance to kick that black dust off my feet and move on. The VA is the God-given foundation I stand on because they never said no when I asked for help. The community of care providers made every effort to provide me with specific programs in efforts to help me identity my demons and learn to live more productively. I did eventually overcome the countless obstacles that kept me bound and am today, made whole. I thank God for allowing me my brokenness to a point I had to own my own and acknowledge my part in my wrongs. Eventually I had to step back and inventory myself because I still had black baggage weighing me down that I needed to discard. Today my black and personal realization of the beauty in my black is innate and genetic as I have learned that I was born beautiful, and born of the female species in this human race and not just born black. With my blackness yet to come full circle, I wonder if we can get back to before I was black, before black became a curse. Can we get back to Negro maybe one day. The definition for Negro in most dictionaries I've read, is a dark skin person, and is the Spanish word for the color black. Black is a mainstay, permanent and a coffee bean to speak, yet there are no white coffee beans if I may. Black still taste dirty in my mouth even though it is a beautiful stockpot of all colors, it rolls off my tongue dirty but I didn't want white anymore. White can be very dirty and illusive at times when it looks clean until you get closer, but my black is bold yet translucent and my black isn't dirty anymore, it absorbs dirt and even reflects it accordingly. Take a paint stroke of white on canvas, and stroke it with black and see what happens. I have become black, proud, loud at times and colorful, with a resounding voice and I am not that angry black woman. If I am angry, I am angry woman…hear me now. My mom always said to us children growing up, to always do and be the best you can because can't nobody do it for you and they won't do it like you do and you never know who watching you. She said if you going to do something, do it for yourself and it will be done right. I'm am yet a work in progress, with a few more black rows to hoe but with determination. Even with my PTSD diagnosis, I felt proud because now I had a treatable diagnosis, a steady and dependable source of income and, consequently

I learned that my behavior was not all my fault, that there were other mitigating circumstances that summoned the demeanor of woman I had become. By the time I got my first lump sum of disability compensation from the VA, I had met and lived with a man, a black man unlike any man I ever dated. He was a country man, sort of raggedy with his flannel shirts and jeans, he was in recovery from alcohol abuse, still strong and virile and most of all, he loved me.

My counselor had warned me not to get romantically with any of the guys in the recovery program as it would be a challenge and probably not good for my sobriety efforts. She was right! Yet I am and was all woman, and most women want the love of a man because we all are flawed and have a past. It was my joy to groom him and bring him up to date with the fashion and lifestyle of today, as he had been living homeless, sleeping in parks and the likes with a bottle in his hand, yet and still, he was just like me, seeking a better way of life and we both were black.

Becoming Black was not so black after all with me and my future husband in a new house with hopes to marry and live happily ever after. Had I known a black ravine was ahead, around the corner, I would probably have waited and learned more about the risk I was undertaking having used most of my compensation award to purchase our home. Arizona has canyons blacker than tar and most overwhelming for me, though I am not afraid of heights, I am afraid of hell. Some of those canyons were just gateways to hell and not for me, breathtaking is exactly what they were. My new home in Prescott Valley was just a stepping stone, but my man was at the height of what he desired in life and most comfortable. This house sat at the base of Superstition Mountains on Superstition Lane and I was just proud as I could be in a long-term relationship and in recovery. It also felt fantabulous to be the only black couple in our neighborhood, yet I was torn, feeling I had finally arrived and realizing I could no longer be that black from hard time Mississippi. I elevated my game, and put to work the greatness already within me with more articulate vocabularies, and refined social engagements. Today's world requires specifics when sharing information or it can be quickly taken out of context. We're living in a take-it-out-of-context genre or generation to speak and nothing is quite as it appears. I always say if it looks like a duck, walks like a duck and quacks like a duck; it's a damn deer. We're receiving multitudes of misleading information on varied and massive platforms and I personally know from experience to check all info from Google and any other search engine again, check it twice or thrice. Fake news is real in every dynamic of our society and it travels on the back of artificial intelligence to the point, no one has to think anymore. Right now, it is just you and I, communicating through the words in this book and it's private, as I can be honest with every word and no context or analysis is needed. Many of the words in the core of this story can be taken out of context easily but this is my truth and truth will set you free as this book is my evidence. My story is mine, my truth is mine and the truth needs no back up; it can stand all on its own. My story dances back and forth with rhythms of vast experiences which is the validation of my honesty and I love it. I wasn't always honest. This is chapter two, Becoming Black of which I've made the decision to accept and become black so it work better for me. Ironically, in Arizona, living in a white neighborhood, in a white state with just a little bit of that white income, translated to me as, I'm finally white. Ouch! This story is just a part of the grand story and it's not his story even though it maps history which has its own dance. The whites I encountered in Prescott were very friendly and inviting and my fiance and I stood out, but in a beautiful way, well-groomed with swagger. Amazingly, I would visit my home state just to feel black again, to be and feel like nigga and socialize with my roots as my new status in life was not black enough. Pay attention to the details. It wasn't the white friends or church members at church we adopted or that adopted us, it was blacks, that got my new love and I off track in our sobriety and our recovery program. I had five years under my belt and my love had two and we were shining bright. Life was amazingly beautiful and happy. I sang in the choir and played a major role helping to establish the first black church that had been in Prescott Valley in over forty years. Let's not forget I'm a Capricorn and status is important to me having been saved from that old miry black clay on that old black river still swamped steeping with those old black ghosts of not-so-black Mississippi.

Becoming Black required a new lesson in preventive maintenance as it only took one joint and one quart of Miller Beer to lead my love and I into a no turning back kind of relapse. Drug addiction is an absolute monster, a beast-like anaconda and as they refer to it in recovery programs, the sleeping tiger and she had awakened and roared loudly. My relapse stripped me of a much-desired five-year love affair and of myself, once again. The details of my new spiral downhill are not as important as the lessons I learned. My relapse was a death sentence with overwhelming shame and guilt. I thought my addiction had been cured but now I had to learn about triggers, environments, people, places and things that threaten recovery all over again. All it took was one joint and a beer to wake up my demons and soon, within a year, I was strung out on crack again while my fiance got introduced to crystal meth and was now addicted to it. We split up and it was the worst heartbreak ever, it was like losing a baby and I cried for two years with a crack pipe in my mouth. It was painful and I was ashamed having gone from sugar to shit in my new white environment. I lived in my truck and got in more trouble with the law, heading back to jail on four different occasions for drugs. The last time I was incarcerated, I was released on probation and I knew I had to get the hell out of Arizona. It's hard and costly to get out of trouble with the law there, and the jails ironically are full of white people and Indians. For some weird and uncomfortable reason, I felt good being one of a few blacks incarcerated. One thing for sure about me was when I got too deep in darkness, I would flee as I got permission from the court to visit my hometown yet, I knew I would never return there. My probation officer said I had to return or a warrant would be issued for my arrest which prompted my internal greatness again as I petitioned to the courts with many letters from home attesting my good behavior. It didn't work and the courts wanted me back in jail but soon God showed up and showed out. The problem now was how to get home as I spent every dime I could muster on crack and had lost my vehicle. I started walking one night headed to the Greyhound bus station thinking I could get a courtesy ticket home. I walked all night, but the bus station manager said they didn't issue courtesy tickets anymore and I was dead. I started crying like a baby not knowing what to do with no place to go but the manager at the bus station, a black woman, made an exception and granted me a guest ticket home; she felt my despair and my fear. She sympathized my distress and God touched her heart as I headed back to Mississippi once again, broken, beaten, and hopeless with black crack clouds still hovering over me. My addiction traveled back home with me and again I was out of control. God moved again in a mighty way as I eventually received a letter from the courts stating my two-year probation period had been satisfied and I was again free. There was a discipline for me to engage with my addiction proving that addiction was just part of the problem. It required me to look at my old black soul. Overcoming my addiction required me go again get my black butt naked before God so those black demons inside could be loosed in heaven. Woe black me.

Becoming Black explored the core of my belief system and that exploration echoed loudly that I was not all I thought I was. I was not the bomb. com and I had yet to discover myself completely. Seeking help from my medical team at the VA, gave me hope and landed me in the Wiser Program at the Michael D. Debakey VA Medical Center in Houston, Texas. I completed another in-patient dual diagnosis recovery program successfully and pursued further sobriety at the Santa Maria Hostel in Spring Branch. With a year of clean time under my belt, I applied and got accepted at the Art Institute of Houston seeking a degree in graphic design. I couldn't give up on little black me, no matter how black my past and I by now, believed and had received my black badge of approval. Most of the female veterans at Santa Maria were friends and almost like family as we looked out and cared for each other. We as a people, are but one community and can always come together in unity for the common good. My black skin I was never ashamed of, but the black poverty and misinformation it implanted in my youth compromised my conception of the bigger world. Houston and Santa Maria both, gave me legs to stand on, as my story had now been enhanced and I had become black woman rather than a black spider. It felt good being black in Houston, with not one recognizable engagement of racism, it seemed the road to success was available to anyone seeking success. Willing to put in the work, I again, was on my way up but as fate would have it, the rain from that black ominous cloud that had been following me all my life was about to wreak havoc upon me like a hurricane. While in my first semester at the Art Institute of Houston, I was standing in line at the bookstore during class break when my face started twitching uncontrollably. It was embarrassing and I had no idea what was causing the twitching but upon arrival back to Santa Maria, my friends there asked me if I was okay because my face had drooped. To this day, I don't know what they saw, but the staff there called the ambulance which took me to Memorial Hermann Hospital where they discovered two brain tumors. Yet this is not of story of woe, but a story of survival, endurance, grace and mercy whereas the best is still yet to come. When the doctors told me what they found, I was flabbergasted and didn't believe them, but when they told me they had to remove the larger tumor immediately, I told them I had to think about it. The only time I remember having fear is when they told me I didn't have time to think about it. Within ten days after being transferred to the Houston VA hospital, the doctors successfully removed a six-centimeter tumor from the right frontal lobe which had caused my brain to swell. The second tumor they discovered on my left frontal lobe is still growing slowly today on my brain and I am eternally grateful that my tumors are meningiomas and not cancerous. Now, on this very day I have three tumors growing on my brain and this knowledge helps me to move forward writing this manuscript for my first book. The Father, The Son and The Holy Spirit are slowly growing in my head and that's how I interpret this affliction because I will not let it hinder me, as it is my miracle. This book, my story is about self-discovery, redemption, restoration and victory and is my testimony of how great God is. I am black today and I am strong today without any apologies. Recovery from the brain surgery was challenging as I lost blocks of memories and I started having grand mal seizures back-to-back, and this put me back in the hospital. Some of the best neurosurgeons in the world were right there in Houston and I knew that God had allowed me to be there where I could get the best of care. When they shaved my head for surgery, I saw many scars on my scalp from previous assaults and I realized just how blessed I was to still be alive, walking and talking. Santa Maria received me back from my hospital stay with open and loving arms. The veterans there, mostly friends of mine, took very good care of me and I applaud them as I could not care for myself with the seizures, but they did and they didn't miss a beat. Eventually, with medicine and my neurotransmitters connecting correctly, I was freed from the seizures and ready to go home, back to Mississippi, to be near family. My gratitude to Houston, the doctors at Michael Debakey, Santa Maria Hostel, and my veteran friends there, is without measure. I am eternally grateful that they were already in place for my journey into the darkness that came with brain surgery. We shall prevail little black girl. With all my sins forgiven and eighteen months of clean time, I didn't give thought to that sleeping tiger of addiction and I moved back home. Within five months home, I was in the crack house again as I heard people say if I smoked it again after brain surgery, it would kill me. Naturally, Cochise the warrior, had to prove them wrong and I did because I'm still here writing my story some eight years later. Black don't crack and I have become black embracing every aspect of my blackness because black doesn't define me. I define me, I define my black, and today I know the definition of who I am, having overcome the many obstacles designed to defeat me. My black is proud today and my black has purpose today. No weapon formed against me has prospered, I am triumphantly grateful and unquestionably blackity, black, black. If that's okay.

CHAPTER THREE

# Black on Purpose

*"Blessed is she who has believed God
would fulfill his promises to her"*

B lack on Purpose is the woman I am today as I am ebony, jet, obsidian, onyx, blackalicious, raven, sable, dusky, nigga black. I am coal, igneous charcoal, Ethiopian, Creole, Blackfoot black. I am inky, midnight, moon shadow black.

I am Japanese black pine, starry, created by design black. My black is strength, powerful, jade, faith, emotional, and jungle black.

My black today is wonderfully beautiful, with boundless purpose and it is not threatening, gloomy, murky, dingy or dim. It is not void nor depressed; it is not stained, parched nor is it dying of thirst. My particular and personalized black is sensuous, embracing, prestigious and warm, it is morning dew and midnight sun. Know and believe my black is not as defined as it is not dark art, black market, black sheep, black magic nor the old black belt struggling in that old black hole. My purpose is the summary totality not only as woman born beautiful, created in the image of God, but as a woman who does not let outside imperatives and adjectives, dictate my own belief system. My entirety and spirit are an assembling of many colorful stories and broken pathways I've had to travel and endure. The color of my skin is not who I am, but my heart and my actions echo who I am. Talk is cheap, but it's the walk that gets you where you're trying to go. Having walked many long dark and black roads to get where I am, my substance is a loving and forgiving heart. I've forgiven every assault made upon me, every medical affliction and every effort made to bound and keep me down. Many of my stories reflect the struggles I endured as a young black girl who could not accept her own skin tone as a negative and thus the realization that skin tones do not define a people. It appeared the poverty we lived was because of a black label whereas today I still have that label but I am rich, rich in spirit, and rich in truth. While writing "Before I Was Black", anger filled my spirit and soul over and over again. The reflections of my truth as a Black, provoked intense emotions that I've been called to share because racism is still alive today and the walls racism has built must come down. These walls are coming down is my prophesy and it will be ugly black. The hurdles I had to jump because of my race are not as difficult today as they were before desegregation. I am no longer that angry black woman and my journey to become this not-so-angry black woman died with the many potholes of truth I learned that were a lie. My black is supremely expressive and rich in culture colored and colorful lingo, jargons and dance, my black waves my hands and will stomp my feet, spit at snakes and grit my teeth. My black is mysterious, curious, no longer furious but it lingers and cannot be denied with hungered pain and silent cries. My poor black people were lied to and the resulting mindset damaged the entire community. The many history books used in the institutions of educations were his story and not our story. We learned to steal to feed families and we learned to manipulate from the same people that has manipulated us for too many years. This book is not an accusation, but a summary of my black experiences and how I overcame all the black hurdles I had to jump to get to my today. I had to prove the greatness within me with the same stamina I had to feed my drug addiction and the ideology that I had to be white to live white, to live a quality life and that has turned out to be a big black lie, a predisposed organized black lie.

Black on Purpose is the dismantling of my youthful beliefs and thoughts that I had to sleep with or marry a white man to be successful in life. It is the affirmation that I am great without cleaning the bathrooms and kitchens of the white community. It is the declaration of self-discovery and growth that afforded my today. My black has a voice and the authority to dispute the truth of the past that purported black people as an inferior race. Not only blacks have had to fight and be killed seeking simple civil rights and liberties, but the entire community of native Indians came under similar scrutiny. The same kind of white people that constructed our government and constitution, are the same as the ones denying the insurrection of our capital. There is a white that I don't like and that is the white that doesn't like me because of my God-given skin color. We have yet to overcome, be viewed and treated as equals even though we have made great stride and are on the way up, we have yet, a long way to go. There will always be racisms as from the days of the Old Testament where money and status were the prerequisites for a decent quality lifestyle. Not all blacks have traveled my path and lived through a physical and relentless racism, but blacks know because someone they know probably their ancestors can bear witness to it. Now that I've observed over six decades of this black experience in its truth, I will be denying a commission of God, an appointment to speak, if I fail to verbalize and document my journey and further fulfill my purpose in Christ. Profound elements of racism still exist in every institution of our great country but those walls are coming down as I believe it is God's Will that they must come down. My life stories are minimalized in this book as I have volumes of stories to share, but they would be too great and not pertinent to my black experience. No one should feel what I felt as a young black girl anywhere in the United States or beyond, and now young white girls are crying when they are shown what racism looked like in America. Racism has no place anywhere in our great country, but that doesn't mean we sweep it under the rug pretending it wasn't a factor in our fight for freedom, liberty, and justice for all. Black history is America's history no matter how dark it may be, it is light.

Black on Purpose validates my truth and what I had to learn to become progressive, mainstream American. A significant portion of my experiences stemmed from the color of my skin. Back when I got the title as the first black news reporter at my hometown newspaper, it was only because another black woman working at the unemployment office whispered in my ear that they were looking for a staff writer over there and she also whispered to me to take the nose ring I wore off, to help my chances. The white woman at the local unemployment office supposedly helping me find employment never said a word because I was black and that disqualified me. I was greatly qualified and every test they gave me to obtain this job at the Columbian Progress

Newspaper, I passed with flying colors. These are the black experiences my story reflects as my life experiences come in various colors. The existence of such parameters and how it affects the mind and self-esteem is crippling and must be conquered. Greatness was within me when I was born, but society had me believing I was not qualified to be great and that I had part the Red Sea to be great. It was okay to be black and poor as long as you remained black and poor is how I interpreted the visible and unequal liberties in our society. Blacks aren't the only sector fighting this battle, all races other than the white race have to battle for equal rights and access to finer living. America is just starting to represent America. From the White House to the poor house, people of all colors, creeds, religions, races and status are being introduced and have become a part of our governing body. One day there will be no need for the label of the first Black, Asian or Latino, because all races have the same capabilities as the predominant race of our country. I don't need a Black History Month to exemplify the greatness, gifts and excellence of my people, but to applaud this designation supports our legacy. It is the legacy that gives hope and build bridges for our future as equals in this country and in our government and it's the legacy that will keep the struggle alive. Black on black crime, police brutality especially against our black brothers, and the imbalanced justice system would become less if we as a people united across the land. My voice will be heard no matter how feeble, nevertheless, when it is united with a million other feeble voices, it will roar like a volcano. There's great power in numbers and the Word of God, says when two or three are gathered in the Name of Jesus, that He will be there also. It still feels like that white that I don't like is yet in control. If my people would like, comment or share the inevitable word of goodness, love and unity like they do on Facebook, Twitter, Instagram, and TikTok, what a mighty nation we could become and behold. There is great division on social media platforms and the voice of racism is ever so strong. I have no regret in my struggle to become black as I was black all along. It was the oppression of the black label upon me, that I regret. The myriad obstacles and afflictions I had to overcome to discover my own greatness as a woman and as a black woman are less but they are not completely resolved. Fear does not exist and has no purpose in my life today as I don't have to cross the street when I see a black cat, nor do I feel as I'm on the blacklist in our country. My black is exact and is full of purpose. The three brain tumors growing slowly in my head coupled with other medical afflictions only sparked the flame to fulfill my purpose. I am no longer the black sheep or ugly duckling chasing a black market under black cloud; I am Black on purpose. I am great on purpose and I will prevail on purpose.

Black on Purpose substantiates my ability and willingness to give back with grace what has been given unto me and will hopefully endorse me to greater heights. I aim to specifically minister and support truth, my truth, no matter what it feels like, in this written and documented act of love. Love is truth, truth is love, truth bears good fruit and good fruit produces good seeds to impregnate the soil of humanity. The truth will set us free. This story of love and the true freedom of expression, is the core of my existence and the only thing I am addicted to today is life and life more abundantly. The remembrance of the many years I traveled dark and dangerous roads all over this country seeking myself, fills my heart will gratitude because I made it. We can all make it to a greater destiny on this earth when we believe. When I returned to Mississippi after my brain surgery and relapsed in 2014, I could've easily given up because I was completely torn down again, and felt like dying, but this is when purpose showed up and pushed me forward. Black on purpose is exposure, transparency and self-awareness and it bears no shame or guilt. I can pat myself on the back, encourage myself and lift myself up as I pursued recovery for the last time and it worked completely. Down in Bay Pines, Florida where I went to my last recovery program, I learned something that will last my lifetime. I learned to manage my thoughts, emotions and behavior including the notion of balance, as my PTSD is yet alive but it does not prosper. With this new information, I returned to college and got my BA degree in studio fine arts from Jackson State University in 2019, graduating magna cum laude and am now a proud homeowner. God knew the plans He had for me and they gave me hope and a future. I am in my future today. The best is yet to come but the here and now has boundless purpose and the greatness I had within me all along has come to the forefront. Acceptance of self is magnanimous and absolutely necessary for inner peace. There's no superior peace than the peace of heart, mind, soul and body collectively. My first few years in this recovery attempt resulted in a few slips and slides, but I refused to let my addiction settle back in as I continue to blossom, like the blackberry bushes on the train tracks at the place of my birth, before I was black, and the black cherry tree still blooming in my mother's backyard. Black on Purpose is the substance of things I hoped for so many days standing on the highway in the middle of the night not knowing which way to go cracked out of my mind. Unwavering faith fed my hope as I fled the man I married as he chased me down the highway in the cold January rain, in my night gown, with blood running down my face. Hope gave me courage to pursue another dawning of day even when at times I was at fault for a few of the battles I fought. After taking many pills to end my life, one year at mother's house, I awakened three days later to find myself still in this old black world. My mom said to me and the words she spoke to me are engraved on my heart as she said, well, you ain't no good at dying, so you might as well live. Momma unknowingly planted seeds in my life that would one day become the roots of which I have flourished. Having learned the hard way that no matter how black the roads we travel, there is light on the horizon if we just lift up our heads and open our eyes. Negative people, places and things will break you only if you let them. I never gave up hope even when I wanted to give up, something deep inside kept me hoping for a better day and less burdens to carry. Sometimes we don't have the strength to bear our own burdens, but there is One who gives us strength and the only One who is made strong in our weaknesses. While in residential treatment at Bay Pines PTSD recovery program, I learned that I had become so accustomed to burying my pain rather than addressing the pain, it had become a defense mechanism of protection. Easily I dismissed my hurt and pain in efforts to move past and forward, but in reality, I was only intombing it and it all remained deep inside. Soon, I had dismissed everyone, to the point I wanted to kill everyone, and that's a dangerous element to have in spirit and it caused me to find myself all alone so many times. We weren't afforded the right to emotions in the olden days and we learned to do as we were told to do without any attachments. Not knowing it was okay to feel bad or to be confused and hurting, caused me to have tunnel vision and look only to myself for help. It takes courage to ask for help and greater courage to recognize the need for help. Today, psychiatry and psychology practices have a module or treatment plan for most mental issues and within these practices, life is not so black after all. Having partake in so many fights and assaults, it was revealed to me that I had anger issues though I've never been violent. Anger, pain and hurt fueled my drug addiction, my eagerness to run away and to not trust anyone. Trust issues are not as big of a problem as before, because I learned to trust God in all my ways, and He has blessed me with great discernment and clarity. I can smell trouble a mile away seeping through the black faced shrubbery of life's meandering highways and byways. My eyes hear very well and my ears can see better than my cataract covered eyes, if that's okay.

Black on Purpose is the evidence of unseen victory, overcoming and jumping over the many hurdles of my life that carried through the grips of death. Information is great nowadays and the gateway to growth as I now have knowledge to make better decisions in my life with the understanding of what choices are made of. Having choices is a blessed institution otherwise life itself would be a prison for many. Jail, prison, domestic violence and my inability to bear children did not break me, but provided me the importance of making more positive choices and it is my gift to self and to this world. If my gift is not opened; it is just a present sitting on the shelf of yesterday. Opening the gift of choice is the supreme element in growth and development as it puts the power of life in our own hands. Ironically, I chose to help the white man find cocaine that landed me a prison under a felony conviction. I chose to answer the call of the white man whom I thought I loved me until he raped me and took away my future as a mother and I chose to marry a man who almost cost me my life. Acceptance and ownership exposed the guilt and shame of my actions and in return I was able to forgive myself and grow on, into more constructive environments. I opened my gift of choice with intelligence and perception thereby, I was made free. Forgiveness of self is priority when closing doors to the past and forgiveness of others will free the spirit and comfort the soul. With purpose I am made whole and I point no fingers to the past as my finger is pointed up, to God Almighty. So many years I looked to blame others for my bad choices and the hell I had to endure, but today I just look in the mirror and there is no blame, no shame, and no fame only goodness of heart has remained. Jackson Mississippi was not my favorite place to be, as I had ugly history with Jackson and had some fear of it, but it worked for me. I was able to solidify my recovery efforts, get a college degree and financial stability and this taught me that things may not be all you desire, but if it works for you, make it work. My first couple of years in Jackson, I felt so much like the potholes that consume the city and like its water, I too needed more purification to speak. While in school at JSU, I wrote a poem for a class, that shares with you the black I once felt:

# I AM JACKSON

I Am Jackson - Black and pasty, haunting and elusive just like the potholes so deep and wringing wet, where calloused racism steeps. Obscured undocumented history of yesterday creep and weeps

I Am Jackson - Strong and secretive alike the old oak hanging trees, mostly dead but still alive and green, dusted with faltering good deeds oppressed with neglected, rejected and timeless needs

I Am Jackson - Deliberate and ghastly similar to the graveyard statues before Tiger Campus, on day to day we meet, twisting, impoverished and thick as the streets everchanging mystique yet void and obsolete

I Am Jackson - Succulent and yielding like the orange pekoe leaves of sweet black Mississippi tea lemon twists and the hungry seasoned black-eyed peas with cornbread violence and segregation at its peak

I Am Jackson - Potholes and rugged, deeper and steeper around the knees they leap, absent in color but rich in tearful agony, furrowed, crumbled and elusive feat powerless to treat, delete and to defeat

I Am Jackson - Reflective and protective of days gone by and days to come, stifled and depressed, without retreat, ugly sticky mud on the bottom feet soaked in guarded inheritance where the red clay leaks

I Am Jackson — Hungry and angry with desires for economic kisses and wishes that have gone to sleep, prosperity and loyalty depletes, incomplete, ablaze with hope, lingering backstreets full of conceit

> I am Jackson - Strong and resilient, buried treasure along that snaky River Pearl, shimmering, glimmering kissed by noonday sun, full of woe, full of hope, longing a tomorrow just to say well done.

Black on Purpose is the development and nourishment of a personal relationship with my Savior and Father God, as the Holy Spirit spoke and ministered that I stop looking around at people and the conditions of this world, but instead to look up and thereby, life became more beautiful. It all started before I was black and in hindsight, the journey was worth the fight, as I am most black, most proud and I am woman. Not white woman, but ironically, not black either, because black doesn't define the beauty of my essence; I do, I will and I shall eternally and most gratefully. If it wasn't for grace and mercy, I couldn't be beautiful as I am today whereas many times, I was so pretty on the outside but black as midnight on the inside. It was at the throne of grace, I stripped down naked and gave everything I had been, all that I was with hopes for all that I could be, to the creator of this Universe. When I was still becoming black, back when I ran the streets of New Orleans, long before crack introduced itself in my life, I eluded death many times and for sure it wasn't me, it was grace and mercy that kept me. One night of survival, hitchhiking from New Orleans back to mom's house in Columbia, a white man gave me a ride and soon as I climbed in his car and shut the door, I immediately knew it was time to get out and quickly. I snatched open my door to jump out, with him reaching behind to me keep me inside his car, when grace and mercy showed up once again and saved me. Now I'm lying on the edge of a swamp in the water holding my breath so the man couldn't find me as he had got out of his car with a flashlight looking for me. God said peace be still and with not one mosquito bite, bruises or cuts, I came out of the water as the white man got back in his car and drove off. My fear and knowledge of that kind of white man made me most skeptical when I was offered a ride by another white man who stopped, saw my condition, all wet, tattered, and greatly afraid. This man took me all the way home with no problem. It instilled in me the idea that all white men are not black on the inside yet, I still call it grace and mercy. Light and darkness lives in all of us and it had nothing to do with race, but what you feed on the inside is what's grow and come out in actions, deeds and words.

Was it resilience or stupidity that I frequent over and over on the dark sides of town or were they lessons and disciplines for me to behold that I may one day, grow old. Black on Purpose is my final answer having given myself over to my innate greatness and the behaviors therein. To go back is to go black but to move up and out is what life is about. I'm so black today I shine.

Black on Purpose ignites my bravery and courage as it denies the probability that I am that old black snake slithering along the old black backroads with black lungs and black tar burnt feet. Neither am I that blackbird whistling black vocals having been blacklisted and blackballed while playing the white man's blackjack. Under the black clouds of life, roaming the blacktop highways of despair and oppression, we bear diminished consequences having defeated that black demon of failure. The blackmailed history of my ancestors black hands of hardship have succumbed to sweet juices of the blackberry as blacker the berry the sweeter the juice. Subsequently the black eyes of abuse have healed and not-so-black vision is birthed with that black magic of the strong black family. Black plagues and blackouts still run rampant in the land under new disguise inclusive of the black market. Blackboards that expose the black hearts of our historical truths in America are yet being wiped clean with black lies. Blackwaters that consume black bodies, blackened by hatred and mistruths are now dry black washouts empty of life. Racism and discrimination, like little blackflies, bite and sting only to fly away and hide. Just like stinky black mold creeping the walls of the shotgun shacks covered with paint, bigotry pretends to never come back. As with the black legs of the black spider, prejudice folds and crawls back into the black holes of disguise. Like the potholes of Jackson, Mississippi, all black and sinister with involuntary intent to cause damage and chaos, discrimination reinvents itself over and over in fear of being lost and lost to the cause. Purpose gives us substance to be who we are without fear, doubt and uncertainty. If there is no purpose in our actions and behavior, what is the purpose in doing the things that we do. Is it curiosity, the sake of experience or a preordained path to our destiny. Having been quiet for way too long, I have a voice today and my voice has purpose. My purpose is to help some weary soul traveling the same roads of my past, to seek, explore and develop the greatness already within. My purpose has set free every day of my past, that I remain free to be all that I can be. My purpose has a tomorrow riding on its back with the lessons of yesterday as my cornerstones and with this manifestation of my calling.

I am she who has believed that God would fulfill His promises to her. I am she who no longer wanders about the land without care. I am she surviving the dangerous highways seeking fortune and fame. I am she not looking for others to blame. I am she come winter, spring, summer or fall. I am she who has answered my call. I am she though disabled and sometime weak. I am she who will get up every day and stand on my feet. I am she no longer a victim or battling within. I am she who will rise and shine again and again. I am she writing this book of redemption and light. I am she who has been blessed with clarity and sight. I am she that is no longer a woman scorned, broken or downcast. I am she who walked the walk and put the past to past. I am she, vibrant, bold and fearless, no longer a slave. I am she with a multitude of memories until the day of my grave. I am she not prideful but ever so proud. I am she, full of culture, not afraid to laugh out loud. I am she with rhythm, energy and a positive vibe. I am she eternally thankful just to be alive.

Black on Purpose is the confirmation that life is no longer a black thang or a white thing, however the struggle continues; it's a life thang and every race has life and strife to behold. Every race has people of ill repute, both good and bad, happy and sad, rich and poor with struggles to endure. Every race has the highs and lows this life will unfold, but truth be told, my black is a gift; it is a treasure more precious than gold. This book is just a portion of my stories, as the stories I have shared in this book, address the issues of misinformation rendered unto me as a black girl growing up not wanting to be black. The educations of my poverty filled youth crippled my mindset and thwarted my growth mentally and emotionally. Yet this is the honest truth of my redemption, restoration, revival and rejuvenation as this truth has more importantly blessed and validated my life with supreme purpose. My purpose today is a pledge of forgiveness and a vow of acceptance which bears no blame to the impoverished misinformation of my youth. It is my declaration of freedom and independence from the troubled choices of my past. It is the epitome and execution of love for myself, for others, and for life. We need purpose in our lives and when we operate with purpose, purpose will reciprocate the efforts we make, which will ultimately glorify the goodness of God. This imperative symbolizes our internal greatness and stabilizes the core of our existence here on earth. We are commanded to the preservation, revitalization and perseverance of humanity. Love is not blind, yet is bears no claim to the racism and divisions that are crippling dynamics of mankind. Love bears witness to truth and the truth stands on its own and needs no explanation. We must learn to love one another no matter what race, color or creed we belong to. Division is a trick of the adversary and it robs from humanity the focus of compassion and concern. We are commanded to love and care for one another. Greatness is within each and every one of us, and greatness is the foundation of all God's creation, and with this greatness of heart, we find peace, goodwill, stamina, endurance and without fail, we find the love we all were created in. My will to survive and comprehend the true meaning of my life is no longer black. It is filled with light, the light of love, laughter and purpose. Every opportunity affording me the display and rhythm of my culture, I embrace with dignity, pride and grace and I thank Almighty God for allowing me this measure of black space. My black, our black is receptive and forgiving, it is a cornerstone, strong and brilliant and it is created in the image of God. My black is the black orchid, the black swan and the black mamba; it absorbs and reflects light and it is a beauty of behold. My black is the symbolic color of solemnity and authority, it is romantic, poetic and it is the rich fertile soil that provide nutrients to our great earth. To everything there is a season; a time for every purpose under heaven. The season is now, for I am black on purpose, and I am a woman of purpose which is the true manifestation and greatness of my journey thus far, in this beautiful world we live in. This is my black story and I'm sticking to it. Thank you for listening. It is well and it is most definitely black.

# ACKNOWLEDGEMENTS AND GRATITUDE

Giving honor and all the glory to God who sustained me, gave me hope for the future, and blessed me with His Word to stand on.

To my brother and mentor, Deacon Ray Charles Oatis, thank you for being a father figure, confidant and for believing in me, encouraging me to go forth and fulfill my dreams with God on my side.

To my nephew, brother and son, Pastor V. Josea Oatis, thank you for igniting the fires of my spirit, lifting me up with your ministry, for never giving up on me and for your kindness and compassion.

To my pastor and friend, Pastor David Daniels and the Friendship M.B. Church, thank you all for your prayers, faith and education in the Word of God for countless years without fail.

To my special mentor, friend and sister in Christ, Dr. Alma Harris, thank you for helping me to define the woman I wanted to become and for blessing me with a voice when I could not speak.

To my sister friend, Sharron Lilly, thank you for your light, for showing me what a good neighbor is in today's world, for your honesty, laughter and for your positive vibes.

To my homegirl and classmate, Phyllis Averett, thank you for continuous inspiration and for providing me the history and timelines of my story with accuracy and without complaint.

CPSIA information can be obtained
at www.ICGtesting.com
Printed in the USA
LVHW041601140723
752116LV00003B/278